the big book of me

Affordable Life Coaching provides the environment and support for you to examine and change your life for the better.

Empowering weekly group sessions around the United Kingdom for individuals and businesses. One-to-one and telecoaching worldwide.

Contact us on +44 (0)207 233 1369 or find out more at www.affordablelifecoaching.org

By bringing the power of life coaching to all, Affordable Life Coaching is revolutionising the life coaching industry.

the big book of me

nina grunfeld

✶ SHORT BOOKS

FIRST PUBLISHED IN 2006 BY

SHORT BOOKS

15 HIGHBURY TERRACE

LONDON N5 1UP

10 9 8 7 6 5 4 3 2 1

A CIP CATALOGUE RECORD FOR THIS BOOK IS AVAILABLE FROM THE BRITISH LIBRARY.

ISBN   1-904977-49-9

PRINTED IN THE UK BY BUTLER AND TANNER LTD, FROME AND LONDON

DESIGNED BY TWO ASSOCIATES

For my family, especially my brother Paul.

conter

Go on, admit that you've opened this book because you're curious.

You may be wondering if this book is for you; you may be wondering what life coaching is all about; you may even be wondering how life coaching could change your life. Just by picking up this book, you've already started coaching yourself, because curiosity is one of the main features of life coaching – getting curious about yourself.

Finding out about ...
- who you are
- what makes you happy
- what motivates you
- what you want from your life
- how to achieve your potential

You are often so busy getting on with your life that you forget about yourself – the 'me' that this book is all about. But time spent on discovering the unique person that you are and what will make you happy – time spent on you – is 100 per cent worthwhile. Once you feel inspired about your life, you will have enough energy, not only for yourself but also for those you love.

No matter what age you are, you'll enjoy *The Big Book Of Me*. It's both for those who are already searching, convinced that there's more to life, and for those who haven't ever thought about their lives before. By working through this collection of practical and inspirational self-development exercises – being curious about who you are – you will begin to understand yourself and define what you want. In each exercise you will discover something you never knew about yourself – something which will make you feel more confident and which you can use towards making your life more as you want it. And, if an exercise doesn't feel relevant to where you are in your life right now, just move on to the next one.

There are seven chapters, which have been designed to work in sequence but can stand on their own if you want them to. Ideally start at chapter one and work through to the end. With each chapter you also complete a Balance Chart, which looks at the whole of your emotional and physical well-being as it stands at present and will help you discover what you want to do next.

As you go through the book, you will learn simple coaching procedures which you'll be able to use to help yourself for ever. You'll find the future you want and unlock what's holding you back from achieving it. You'll find yourself starting to take control of your life and getting ready for whatever you want – including relationships.

Take it easy. Complete the book in bite-size chunks. Ten minutes a day (maybe last thing at night or first thing in the morning) is about right – or more if you feel like it. And if you start working through the book and then forget about it for a few months, don't worry about that either. It's your own life coaching course – enjoy it. Changing your life takes time – as does getting to know yourself. Most of us never take this much time to think about ourselves. It's intense work and you may find that as you work through the book your answers get deeper and more honest. Re-write early anwers. Keep adding information about yourself. Take time to assimilate your new knowledge. And, although this book has been written to take you through the next six months, it does not need to be done to such a specific timeframe. Far better to do it thoroughly than to rush it.

Whenever you come across a specially recorded visualisation or talk that's on the Affordable Life Coaching website (www.affordablelifecoaching.org), log on and listen. Hearing some of our guidance actually spoken will deepen your knowledge and understanding.

The Big Book Of Me is for you. As you complete these exercises you will be totally honest, because only you need ever see what you've written – and because, if you're not totally honest, you won't learn anything about yourself. If friends want to see what's inside, read some of the questions out to them and then suggest they get their own copy and you can work through the exercises together. You may find it more fun with a friend. Or, better still, come to Affordable Life Coaching and get the support of a group of people who are all keen to change something to improve the quality of their lives.

When you've finished *The Big Book Of Me*, you'll probably say – 'If only I'd known this before'. But it's not too late. It's a book that will change your thinking forever. Start now. Get even more curious.

'And the day came when the risk to remain tight in a bud was more painful than the risk it took to blossom.'

Anais Nin

1
Coaching **tools**

Who Are You?

Before you start learning how to coach yourself, take a few minutes to fill in your first Balance Chart, which you'll find opposite. As you work through *The Big Book of Me* you'll be working with your Balance Chart a lot – and you'll enjoy filling it in and watching yourself change.

What's My Balance Chart For?

You can use it to :

● focus yourself on what to do in order to change your life – the areas with the lowest scores will probably be the areas you'd want to start setting goals about first.

● instantly see the way your life is changing – by comparing one of your Balance Charts to the next, you'll notice the changes in your life at once.

● see whether you're living your life according to your goals – if your goal is to see more of your children and your 'family' segment has scored low, you are probably not honouring that goal; if your goal is to make a lot of money and your 'money' segment scored low, you're probably not achieving that goal – and so on.

filling in my balance chart

My Balance Chart

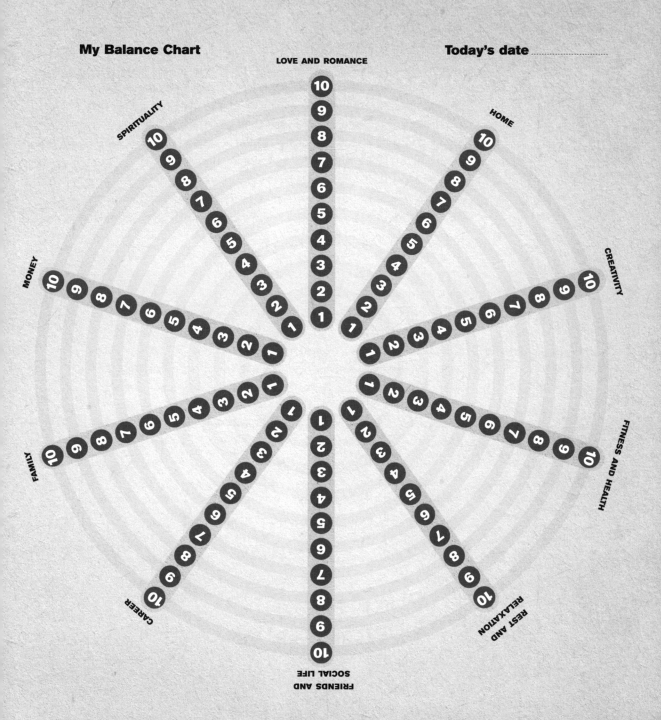

15

Using Your Balance Chart

Be totally honest with yourself when filling in your Balance Chart. You may find this difficult at first, but as you go through the book and start thinking about yourself and your life with greater clarity you will find it will become easier. Your Balance Chart will probably change each time you fill it in (there is a Balance Chart at the beginning of every chapter): this is a natural part of the process of moving forward.

Think about each of the ten sections in turn and give yourself a score according to how satisfied you are at this very moment with that part of your life. The scale runs from 1 (very dissatisfied) to 10 (very satisfied). Circle the relevant numbers; when you have completed all ten sections you can join the numbers to give a personal shape that expresses the way you feel about your life today. This will focus you on which areas to work on first.

The scores you give yourself on your Balance Chart are an opportunity to improve your life. See them as something to be pleased about or as a challenge, rather than feeling despondent about any low scores you may have. Some of you will naturally use lower numbers rather than higher ones. We all see life – and our own lives – differently and some of us will be generous in our markings when we actually feel the same about our life as someone who uses smaller numbers.

What is important is that you are doing what you want to do, that your life is reflecting your dreams. As you read through *The Big Book of Me*, you'll be finding out how to do just that.

If you want more detailed guidance on filling in your Balance Chart, you can listen to the explanatory introduction on our website (www.affordablelifecoaching.org) or read 'Aspects of Life' (opposite).

Aspects Of Life

Each segment of the Balance Chart is about a different aspect of your life. Make the Balance Chart your own – and remember to date it. If you feel you'd like to add more spokes to your chart, do – it's your life. For example, some people find it impossible to think about their children and their parents as part of the same family and want to divide that segment into two: you may have others you want to divide.

Within each aspect of your life there are lots of things to consider. You will know what each segment means to you, but here are some pointers. Read each aspect as you come to it on your Balance Chart.

Love and Romance
- Expectations (are your expectations too high/too low?)
- Commitment (are your desires compatible with your partner's?)
- Self-love (do you feel worthy of love?)
- Sexuality (are you aware of and ready to accept yours?)
- Sex (do you feel comfortable about sex? are your needs the same as those of your partner?)
- Relationship patterns (do you always pick the same type and have the same sort of relationship?)

Home
- Neighbours (do you get on well or badly?)
- Expenses (can you afford a/your home and related expenses?)
- Location (do you enjoy the area where you live or does it unsettle you in any way?)
- Atmosphere (are you pleased to get home?)
- Light/space (is there enough light and space for you?)
- Other people (do you get on with the people you share your home with? do you have enough privacy?)

Creativity

- Confidence (are you confident about your creativity?)
- Work/life balance (do you have time to be yourself outside work?)
- Talents (are you aware of your talents?)
- Training (would you like to take courses to help you access your creativity?)
- Self-expression (do you know how to express yourself? are you doing so?)

Health and Fitness

- Addictions (if you have any addictions, are you dealing with them?)
- Exercise (are you getting enough exercise? do you know what exercise you enjoy? are you exercising too much?)
- Diet (are you eating healthily and respecting your body?)
- Self-image (do you have a positive self-image of yourself?)
- Routine maintenance (do you have regular check-ups – doctor, dentist, hygienist etc?)

Rest and Relaxation

- Sleeping arrangements (is your bed comfortable and your room relaxing?)
- Stress/tension (do you often feel stressed?)
- Holidays (do you take regular holidays? can you relax on holiday?)
- Insomnia (do you have many sleepless nights?)
- Sleep disturbance (do you frequently wake during the night?)

Friends and Social Life

- Availability (do you have time for your friends and do your friends have time for you?)
- New friends (do you make new friends?)
- Intimacy (can you be intimate with your friends? do you have friends you can confide in or do they just confide in you?)
- Old friends (do you enjoy your old friends or have they passed their sell-by date?)
- Variety (do you have friends from a diversity of backgrounds?)

Career

- Career development (is your career developing the way you would like it to? are you in the right field? do you know what you would like to do?)
- Job satisfaction (do you enjoy going to work or is it a chore?)
- Income (are you paid enough?)
- Relationships (do you have good relationships at work?)
- Performance (do you feel well qualified enough for your job or would you like to do further training?)
- Working environment (does your company have the same values as you do? are there decent facilities?)

Family

- Parents (are you good friends with your parents or do you blame them for everything that's gone wrong in your life?)
- Siblings (do you enjoy each other's company or perhaps you are not on speaking terms?)
- Feuds (are you feuding with in-laws, step-parents, extended family or even family closer to home?)
- Children (do you love your children or feel bogged down by them?)
- Bereavement (are you coping with the loss of a family member?)
- Carer (are you looking after your family?)

Money

- Debt (do you have enough money or are you constantly in debt?)
- Charity (do you give money to charity or to help others?)
- Saving (do you manage to save? do you know what to do with your savings or would you like to be better informed?)
- Spending (do you spend on items you need or anything you fancy and then regret it?)
- Sharing (do you find it difficult to share your money with your family and/or friends?)
- Thrift (would you call yourself mean or over-generous?)

Spirituality

- Religion (do you have a religion and, if not, do you feel the lack?)
- Faith (do you have faith that you are being looked after?)
- Gratitude (are you aware and grateful for everything that you have?)
- Love (do you feel love for others and a connection to them?)
- Purpose (have you found your sense of purpose in the world?)
- Meditation (do you meditate?)
- Trust (do you trust that everything will be alright?)

Now you have understood all the segments in your Balance Chart, you can fill it in. Remember you are filling it in according to how you feel about now – this moment of your life.

Coaching Yourself

Once you've completed your Balance Chart, it's easy to see that you have aspects of your life that you would like to change. It may be that these are very simple things that are comparatively easy to accomplish or it may that you would like to change everything about your life – home, partner and career.

Life coaching starts with the now – what your life is like right this minute and works from here forwards. Begin by changing the way you see yourself. Start noticing the good things about yourself and your life and writing them down. Becoming aware of everything positive that happens to you will increase both your confidence and your optimism. You will find it easier to set goals and, as the weeks go by, you'll make your goals more challenging.

In this chapter you'll also find out about how – if you let it – your mind can stop you from moving forward and you'll work out the values that will help you discover what you want from your life. There are lists of life coaching questions to help you access your intuition and an introduction to the LIFE Model, a unique problem-solving system. What are you waiting for?

going for it

Goals & Achievements

Choosing your goals

Each week, set yourself at least one specific goal. Make it something you can do. Choose a goal which is manageable and achievable, but which you may have been putting off doing. It could be a little scary or even something extremely boring that you have to do.

Ignoring parts of your life that aren't working won't make them go away and you'll feel better about yourself once you start tackling them. No matter how small your step – make it your goal and do it. And then pat yourself on the back.

Once you get used to goal-setting you may want to increase the number of goals you work on each week. You could include one which works towards your life goal and another which is simply fun or relaxing and another which involves more serious work on yourself in the area of your Balance Chart where you scored the lowest. Are you fed up with your job? Do something about it. Are you looking for a partner? Do something about it.

Over the next few pages there are 6 months' worth of goals for you to fill in. By the time you've completed these you will have got yourself in the habit of goal-setting. Choose your goals with care – you will feel a sense of achievement once you've accomplished them.

Noting Achievements

As you begin to list your achievements every week, you'll become more aware of them and will start noticing how your life is changing. It's so easy to think that you haven't achieved anything during the week – especially if you don't achieve your goal, but there are always things that you have achieved, without even noticing it. Even if you are ill in bed, you may have read a book or taken the chance to think something out that you hadn't before. If events overtake you one week and you can't complete your goal, don't worry. Do it next week, or break it into smaller, more manageable goals. Instead of berating yourself, start becoming conscious of your successes.

Goal for week beginning   Date................................

Achievement for week beginning   Date................................

Goal for week beginning   Date................................

Achievement for week beginning   Date................................

Goal for week beginning   Date................................

Achievement for week beginning   Date................................

Goal for week beginning   Date................................

Achievement for week beginning   Date................................

time for your weekly goal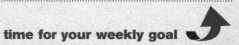

Goal for week beginning .... Date...........................

Achievement for week beginning .... Date...........................

Goal for week beginning .... Date...........................

Achievement for week beginning .... Date...........................

Goal for week beginning .... Date...........................

Achievement for week beginning .... Date...........................

Goal for week beginning .... Date...........................

Achievement for week beginning .... Date...........................

Goal for week beginning

Date...........................

Achievement for week beginning

Date...........................

Goal for week beginning

Date...........................

Achievement for week beginning

Date...........................

Goal for week beginning

Date...........................

Achievement for week beginning

Date...........................

Goal for week beginning

Date...........................

Achievement for week beginning

Date...........................

did I really do all that?

Goal for week beginning .... Date.........................

Achievement for week beginning .... Date.........................

Goal for week beginning .... Date.........................

Achievement for week beginning .... Date.........................

Goal for week beginning .... Date.........................

Achievement for week beginning .... Date.........................

Goal for week beginning .... Date.........................

Achievement for week beginning .... Date.........................

' You are today where the thoughts of yesterday have brought you and you will be tomorrow where the thoughts of today take you..'

Blaise Pascal, French philosopher

Goal for week beginning .... Date ....

Achievement for week beginning .... Date ....

Goal for week beginning .... Date ....

Achievement for week beginning .... Date ....

Goal for week beginning .... Date ....

Achievement for week beginning .... Date ....

Goal for week beginning .... Date ....

Achievement for week beginning .... Date ....

Goal for week beginning   Date.............................

Achievement for week beginning   Date.............................

Goal for week beginning   Date.............................

Achievement for week beginning   Date.............................

Goal for week beginning   Date.............................

Achievement for week beginning   Date.............................

Goal for week beginning   Date.............................

Achievement for week beginning   Date.............................

aim for two goals this week

Goal for week beginning   Date...............................

Achievement for week beginning   Date...............................

Goal for week beginning   Date...............................

Achievement for week beginning   Date...............................

Goal for week beginning   Date...............................

Achievement for week beginning   Date...............................

Goal for week beginning   Date...............................

Achievement for week beginning   Date...............................

Feeling Your Worth

We are all unique individuals with our own strengths and not to be compared. Many of us assume that if we can do something, anyone else can do it. But it just isn't true; not everyone can do the things you can do.

As well as your weekly achievements, think about what you have achieved so far in your life. Feel proud of yourself. Let your confidence grow through realising just what you have accomplished in your life already – and this is only the beginning. If at first you can't think of many achievements don't worry; as you start thinking about your life, more will come to you – and you'll become aware of achieving more too.

If you haven't already, it's very useful to start a record of achievements file and collect together all the certificates you already have or anything which records your successes – as well as anything you feel proud of. Your file could include photographs of you at the top of the mountain or the clay pot you made at school or being handed your first gold medal. It may come in useful in the future and it might also make you realise just how much you've accomplished so far.

Feeling good about yourself and realising your strengths will start you thinking where else you can apply your talents. Begin thinking about the qualities you possess and how to maximise them in all aspects of your life.

you are beginning to live in the world of possibilities

I Am The Greatest

List 5 or more of your achievements
They can be big or small, personal or work related. They could involve doing your first handstand in the swimming pool (especially if you could never do one at school), mastering the computer, getting a qualification, bringing up your children, receiving your first cheque for doing something you love.

Then, think about those achievements
What qualities (e.g. sensitivity, humour, single-mindedness) did you need to achieve them? For example, that first underwater handstand will have taken perseverance, courage, positive thinking.

Now write down how you could apply those qualities to the other areas of your life
For example, perseverance means that if you don't give up, you could finish the book you started to write, but have stuck on the shelf; courage means that you could ask your boss if you could go on a course; positive thinking means you could do other things you always thought you couldn't – like a handstand on land.

My achievements	What qualities did I need?	Where else could I apply these qualities?

Limiting Beliefs

Remembering your achievements will help boost your confidence, but now you want to become curious about the way you think about yourself and the way you limit your potential.

Limiting beliefs can be about anything – and they hold you back and crush your confidence. Notice all those negative phrases – 'I can't…'; 'I'm no good at…'; 'I don't know…'; 'I don't like…'; 'They don't like me…'; or even 'I'll try…' that go running through your brain. Those are the limiting beliefs (or negative assumptions) that you hold about yourself, or others, or about the world, or about the possibility of change.

We use phrases like these all the time – either thinking them to ourselves or even saying them out loud. If you believe, for example, that you can't learn new things – that thought is going to limit you and will stop you learning new things, which in turn will limit you further. Your own thoughts hold you back from achieving your potential.

Overcoming limitations, step by step, will encourage you to take on bigger challenges. Believe in yourself. Think positively – it's such a powerful tool. You know you can do it.

Changing can be challenging, but you've already jumped the first two hurdles:

1. Realising you want to change
2. Buying this book to help you

12 Ways To Get Rid Of Your Limiting Beliefs

1. **Notice your limiting beliefs.** You can only change them once you've identified them.

2. **Contradict your mind.** Each time you become aware of your mind saying 'I can't' or limiting your actions and beliefs – consciously say 'Yes, I can' or 'I am …' – and believe it. If you stop using a pattern it will become weaker and weaker.

3. **Be as flexible as you can about everything** - including the day ahead. You can create anything you want to for your day.

4. **Put incentives back into your life.** Ask yourself what you would really like to do that your limiting beliefs are stopping you from doing. Once you know what you'd really like to do, it'll be an incentive to change.

5. **Act 'as if' you don't have that belief any more.** Up to a point we are all actors. Fake it until it becomes natural.

6. **Use affirmations and positive visualisation** (see pages 101-4). They are both core aids in getting rid of limiting beliefs.

7. **Model your behaviour on someone you would like to be like, or admire.** Ask them to mentor you. Interview them. Find out how they overcame their limiting beliefs.

8. **Be around happy, positive, inspirational people.** It's healthier than being around negative people who may add to your limiting beliefs.

9. **Take risks.** Each week do something you haven't done before – set yourself a goal that really challenges you. Keep taking small steps forward.

10. **Magnify the pain.** Become aware of the costs of not changing your behaviour. Imagine working for your boss for another year or staying forever in the bad relationship you're in now.

11. **Imagine achieving your life goal.** How will you feel when you've achieved it? Thinking of your achievements will spur you on to change.

12. **Act as if this new future had happened.**

making new beliefs

Old Beliefs v. New Beliefs

Give yourself some new beliefs about yourself. Add to the list below.

Old Limiting Belief	New Productive belief
eg I'm hopeless at sport	I love rowing
eg I'm bad at maths	I could take an MBA
eg I'm tone deaf	I'm starting singing lessons
eg I hate change	Every change I've made has been for the better

'Those who
cannot change
their minds
cannot change
anything.'

George Bernard Shaw

Making Progress

You may keeping your limiting beliefs because they suit you. They stop you from having to do certain things that you may not want to do and generally 'protect' you. But dropping your limiting beliefs doesn't mean changing everything about yourself, it simply means not denying yourself your full potential. Decide now which aspects of your limiting behaviour you want to keep and which you want to let go of.

Ask yourself the following questions with each of your limiting beliefs (see page 36).

Old limiting belief and new productive belief I want to work on

....

Benefits I would gain from having this new productive belief

1. ....

2. ....

Benefits I would lose from giving up my old limiting belief

1. ....

2. ....

What excuses do I make as to why I don't change?

....

Go for it! What have you got to lose?

Love/Hate Feelings

Whether or not you are aware of them, your values already govern your life. Becoming aware of them will help you know what you want from your life – and what you don't. Decisions will become easier to make.

Thinking about the questions below will lead you to your values because they will enable you to become aware of the things that move or upset you the most. Everything you love or hate relates to your values. If, for example, you dislike seeing people wearing red noses, dignity may be one of your core values. And, if you dislike people who feel like, that it may be because open-mindedness is one of your values.

Without thinking, or judging yourself, write down as quickly as you can the answers to these questions. Be as honest as you can.

What annoys you about/on TV (think of reality TV, red nose day, the News, advertisements, soaps etc)?

....

....

What annoys you about your partner/friends/family/colleagues?

....

....

What do you admire about partners/friends/family/colleagues?

....

....

how values work

Understanding Your Values

Values are at the heart of your judgement and your behaviour. Becoming aware of your values will strengthen your trust in yourself and your confidence.

Knowing what your values are will –
- help you make decisions
- help you choose the right career
- help you become aware of your identity

Everything that means a lot to you – everything you would fight to preserve, stems from your own personal value system. For example:

If your value is ...	You will live your life ...
honesty/integrity	...without compromising what you say or do ... saying what you think
generosity	... as the giver in relationships, happily giving your money, time and energy
independence	... asking and expecting little from other people

You will have values about :
1. Your inner self and how you arrange your life
2. Your faith and customs
3. How you relate meaningfully to others in social situations
4. How you work and relate to others in your work environment

Which Values Are Yours?

Having thought about your values, circle those values that you recognise as yours and add any others that you can think of.

balance	generosity	moderation	sensitivity
boldness	honesty	modesty	stability
bravery	honour	open-mindedness	tact
calmness	humorousness	order	tenacity
cleanliness	independence	positivity	thrift
considerateness	industriousness	privacy	tolerance
courage	integrity	reliability	trust
creativity	kindness	respectability	truthfulness
decisiveness	loyalty	responsibility	vitality
dignity	magnanimity	self-discipline	wisdom

When you have decided on your values, think about the way you are living your life and the decisions you have taken during your life. Can you see how your values have influenced those decisions? Think about which values have influenced which decisions.

....

....

....

Are you happy with: your career? your partner? your friends? your colleagues? Do they have similar values to you?

....

....

....

'Open your arms to change, but don't let go of your values.'

Dalai Lama

Discovering What You Want

Now you've found your values, you can begin discovering what you want from your life. Asking yourself the right kind of questions will help you to understand exactly who you are and exactly what you'd enjoy doing.

There are two main types of questions – those that keep you blocked with your problem and those that get you in touch with your intuition, change the way you're thinking and move you forward. Too often, our questions are of the first kind, not the second.

Questions that keep you blocked	Questions that move you forward
Why am I sad?	What will make me happier?
Why can't I solve this crossword?	How can I solve this crossword?
Why didn't he kiss me?	How can I get him to kiss me?
Why don't I get promoted?	What can I do to get promoted?
What should I do?	What do I want?

Life coaching questions are forward-moving. They will challenge you, free up your intuition and existing knowledge, help you understand what you're thinking and feeling and focus on solutions.

As your brain is always trying to find an answer to a question, it is better to ask the right question.

What do I want?

Discover what it is that you want, rather than asking what you should do or ought to do. As a general question, ask 'What do I want?' and if that feels too big a question, ask it regarding a particular, specific situation. For example, 'What do I want my birthday party to be like?' or 'What do I want to do about my over-eating?' You'll know the answer.

questions for me

Useful Questions

Throughout *The Big Book of Me* you'll come across different life coaching questions you can use in various situations. Below are some of the most frequent. Turn to this page whenever you have something you're not sure about – and see if you can use these questions on a friend next time they ask your advice.

- Could I avoid this situation another time?
- What would I do differently next time?
- What has to happen for me to feel successful?
- What have I learned about myself from this experience?
- What is my dream for the future?
- What am I not facing up to in this situation?
- What other choices do I have?
- What would happen if I did nothing?
- What haven't I asked that I should ask?
- What can I do to make myself happy right now?
- What do I hope to achieve by doing that?
- What would make the biggest difference to my career/relationship/family/life?

If you like you can embellish your questions :
- If I pretended I knew the answer, what would I say?
- If I could wave a magic wand and grant myself anything I wanted, what would it be?
- On a scale of 1-10, how much do I want to do that?

Jot down any questions you find particularly useful to help you remember them for the future.

....

....

....

'Most teachers waste their time by asking questions which are intended to discover what a pupil does not know, whereas the true art of questioning has for its purpose to discover what the pupil knows or is capable of knowing.'

Albert Einstein

What Do I Want From My LIFE?

The LIFE Model is the main tool life coaches use to help you think about an issue. It will give you an understanding of the issue you want to tackle and of your emotions towards it. You'll find yourself using the LIFE Model every time you have a problem you want to solve – and you'll use it throughout *The Big Book of Me*.

The LIFE Model is a logical sequence of questions that you ask yourself in order to bring out your true feelings (see also the Useful Questions on p.44). When you reach the end of the questions – including any you want to add yourself, you'll have solved your own problem.

You may not have a specific problem you want help with solving at the moment, so you may not want to use the LIFE Model now. Just remember where to find it for when you do want it. If you do have a problem you want solved, begin the LIFE Model by stating your problem. Then work through the four parts of the LIFE Model (Living, Ideal, Fuel and Energy), asking yourself the relevant questions in each part. You can ask as many questions as you like in each part. Below are just a few suggestions.

The L of LIFE stands for Living

'Living' is now – your *current* situation. Before solving your problem, define as honestly as you can what it is. Often just by describing the situation clearly – rather than what you thought or imagined it was – the way forward becomes obvious and straightforward.

These are some examples of 'Living' questions you might like to use :

- What is the problem I would like solved?
- What have I tried so far?
- What's happened to date?
- What other factors are relevant?
- What would I do if I knew I couldn't fail?

The I of LIFE stands for Ideal

'Ideal' is your ideal outcome or goal. Ideally you should be able to measure whether it has been achieved.

These are some examples of 'Ideal' questions for you to use

- What would my 'Ideal' be?
- Why do I want to achieve it?
- Is it within my capabilities and budget?
- Is my 'Ideal' realistic?

Now, write a paragraph describing your goal as if you had already achieved it. For full effect, write it in the present tense.

The F of LIFE stands for Fuel

Fuel is when you think about what options and resources you have at your disposal to help you achieve your 'Ideal'.

These are examples of 'Fuel' questions to help you think of your options:

- What time, money, training, experience, advice, information etc. from others (or myself) will I need in order to achieve my ('Ideal') goal?
- What could I do differently in order to achieve my 'Ideal'?
- What opportunities already exist to help me realise my 'Ideal'?
- How could I create new opportunities in my life?
- What alternatives are there to that approach?
- What option would I most like to act on?
- What would happen if I did nothing?'

The 'E' of LIFE stands for Energy

The final part of the LIFE Model is when you convert the 'Fuel' into 'Energy' and go for it, when you take that first step and commit to action.

A few examples of 'Energy' questions:

- What are my next steps?
- Where and when will I take my next steps?
- How will I know when I've reached my 'Ideal'?
- How committed am I to this 'Ideal'?
- How will I feel when I've achieved it?

Now take that first step towards achieving your goal.

'It isn't that they can't see the solution. It is that they can't see the problem.'

G.K. Chesterton

Coaching Tools is all about …

working out where I am in my life
discovering the multi-faceted me
noting my achievements
setting myself goals
re-thinking me
shedding my old skin
the new me
what I value
learning about me
asking the right questions
getting myself organised
knowing how to achieve my goal

future me

2

futureme

Your Balance Chart

Now you are equipped with some coaching tools and have begun to get curious about who you are and what you want, you are ready to think about the rest of your life. Before beginning the next chapter, complete and date your Balance Chart.

Listen to the explanatory introduction on our website (www.affordablelifecoaching.org) or refer back to the last chapter for instructions on how to fill in your chart. Compare this Balance Chart with the first one you filled in. What changes have you already made?

how satisfied am I?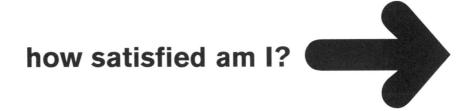

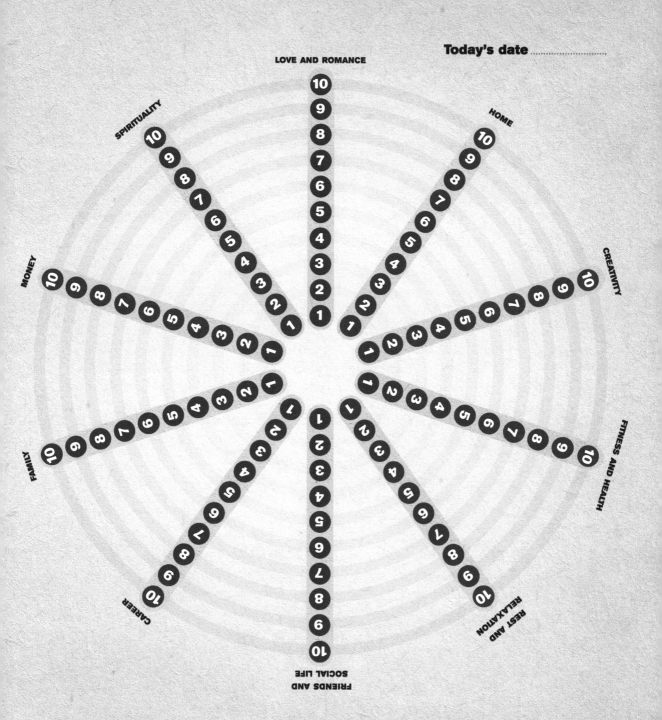

Today's date ....

Finding Your Talents

Your talents are the things that you have a natural ability for, the things which you are drawn to and which make you feel happy when you are doing them. They are not necessarily the things you are good at doing – those are your skills, though they may be your talents as well. Before you can work out what you really want from your life, take stock of what your talents are, so you can build on them.

You can easily see the talents of friends, yet it can be difficult to see your own. You may think that you haven't got any talents; they may have been inadvertently squashed by parents and teachers who haven't understood you. But talents aren't squashed forever; they're waiting to be discovered.

There are several ways to start finding your talents. If your friends and family are open, you can ask them what they remember about you in the past, who they think you are now and what they value you for. You can also listen to your intuition and start noticing each time you have an urge to do something. It may be that you suddenly think, 'I wish I could paint that' or 'I'd love to go deep-sea diving' or 'I could design a room like that'. These urges may well be guiding you to talents you haven't yet expressed. Listen to your fantasies, too. If you aspire to something exotic, there may be a potential talent there, too.

Some of you may already be working in the field you've always loved, but even so you may not be incorporating all your talents into your life.

Our talents may be incorporated into themes that each of us have running through our lives. These themes could be :

- a love of helping others
- colour
- the sea
- collecting

Your themes and the way you express them are uniquely yours. Discover them – they will lead you to your future.

There is an inspirational talk and visualisation on our website (www.affordablelifecoaching.org) which will help you to access your talents.

After you've listened to the visualisation make a note of anything that you enjoyed as a child, as a teenager or in your early twenties. Then write down what you especially loved about each activity.

Things I loved as a child
(eg cycling adventure/freedom/speed)

What I especially loved about each activity

Things I loved as a teenager
(eg ski-ing/friends/speed/cold air)

What I especially loved about each activity

Things I loved in my early 20s
(eg trekking/friends/travel/outdoors)

What I especially loved about each activity

Loving animals does not mean you have to be a vet

Can you see any linking themes between all the things you loved? The example above shows someone sociable, who likes being outdoors and having a sense of freedom. You can see the talents they might have. Similarly, the themes running through your life will lead to your talents.

If you love animals you could photograph dolphins, work for the RSPCA, design cuddly toys, present nature programmes on television, work with guide dogs for the blind, train animals to be film stars, be a zoo keeper, run a kennels or simply think about getting a pet. Think about your passions in as open a way as possible.

Inspirational Moments

There are times in all our lives when we have a sudden revelation or insight that gives our life greater clarity and when we become one with the moment. It's great to remember these experiences as they don't happen very often. They may come when you're listening to stunning music; or scoring a goal; or looking at a beautiful view; or painting a picture; or playing with a child; or reading a book; or riding a horse – or at any other time. These are moments to treasure because they hold the key to who you are, the key to your future. They will also help you to discover what your talents are.

Begin recording them now here and keep adding to them.

Date:	Inspirational Moment – what was I doing?

' Use what talents you possess; the woods would be very silent if no birds sang there except those that sang best.'

Henry Van Dyke, American author

Creating Your Ideal Life

Each of us has a different idea of what a perfect existence would be. A long, white sandy beach may appeal, but then again it may be your idea of total hell. Only you know; only you can create your own ideal life.

Before you begin to create it, start by making your present life as ideal as it could be. You may want to ensure you always have a good book on the go or build in a weekly trip to the cinema or a regular game of tennis. Become aware of what makes your life feel good – and build those things in.

Find out what energises you, gives you confidence, makes you happy. Get curious about what you like. Be aware of yourself during the day and keep checking in to see whether or not you're doing what you want.

Notice:

- **Which people light you up when you talk to them**
- **What activities you enjoy** (*eg swimming in the sea, catching falling leaves, riding your motorbike*)
- **What for you is a treat** (*eg a glass of champagne, a massage, going to bed with a good book*)
- **What energises you?** (*eg drinking water, dancing, having a nap*)
- **What makes you feel good** (*eg singing along with the radio, watching a fire, feeding the ducks*)
- **What stretches your mind in different directions** (*eg learning the piano, helping out at a charity, reading this book*)
- **What hobbies you enjoy** (*eg writing poetry, riding, cooking*)

All these things can be built in to your ideal life – starting now.

This is not selfish. Working towards giving yourself your ideal life will make you a calmer, more generous, more loving person and will both relax and energise you.

By concentrating on your present life and perfecting it, you may even find you don't have to make any major adjustments – you are happy as you are.

Date

My Enjoyment Diary: Day 1

Every day for a week write down each day what you really enjoyed about that day and what you would have liked to have changed about that day.

What I really enjoyed about today

What I would have liked to have changed about today

Date

My Enjoyment Diary: Day 2

....

What I really enjoyed about today

....

What I would have liked to have changed about today

Date   **My Enjoyment Diary: Day 3**

....

What I really enjoyed about today

....

What I would have liked to have changed about today

what a great day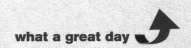

Date

My Enjoyment Diary: Day 4

What I really enjoyed about today

What I would have liked to have changed about today

Date

My Enjoyment Diary: Day 5

What I really enjoyed about today

What I would have liked to have changed about today

I'm noticing the good things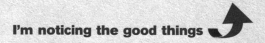

Date
My Enjoyment Diary: Day 6

....

What I really enjoyed about today

....

What I would have liked to have changed about today

Date

My Enjoyment Diary: Day 7

....

What I really enjoyed about today

....

What I would have liked to have changed about today

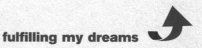

fulfilling my dreams

Unfulfilled Dreams

As well as making your present life closer to your ideal, and discovering your talents and passions, think about any unfulfilled dreams you have.

1. Opposite, write a list of things you've always wanted to do.
This list is one of the keys to your future. It could be that from now on you might actively decide to pursue at least one of those dreams, or it could be that without realising it you are already doing so.

Whether you've always wanted to travel round the world or get a degree or live by the seaside or collect beer mats, write a list of all the dreams that to date you haven't fulfilled. Instead of vague aspirations like 'I'd like to be rich' or 'I'd like to be happy', put down specific dreams, like 'I'd like to be a doctor' or 'I'd like to build my own house'.

2. Think about each of those dreams on your list and work out what the fulfilment of that dream represents to you.
What if you had achieved your dream? What was it about that dream that you really wanted? Be as honest and specific as possible.

For example, wanting to live by the seaside might represent a desire to swim every day, or to have the feeling of being on an eternal holiday or to have the freedom we associate with the beach. Wanting to build your own home, for example, might mean you want to see something concrete grow, or that you want to create something permanent and beautiful.

3. How could you achieve the same results in another way?
Once you have realised that your dream may be symbolic of something you are already achieving, or could easily be achieving, it makes it much easier to take that first step towards your new future.

For example, if it is the feeling of freedom that you want, maybe you could achieve that in your life – by working freelance or travelling more. Or, if you want to create something permanent and beautiful, why not a garden or a painting or a piece of furniture or a business?

Things I've always wanted to do	Why I want to do them	In what other way could I achieve the same results

The hope of fulfilling your unfulfilled dreams can keep you feeling alive and positive about the future, but it is also wonderfully satisfying to realise that your life has not gone off on the wrong tangent after all and that some of your dreams are actually being fulfilled – or could easily be.

For example, if you have gone through life always regretting not having become a doctor, you might find that if, for example, you went to work at the local university canteen your dream of being a doctor would vanish because being at the canteen would fulfil it. You'd be with people all the time, seeing them, listening to them, there for them.

Once you work out what it is about that dream that you really crave, you are on your way to being able to achieve it.

'A man who does not plan long ahead will find trouble right at his door.'

Confucius

Working Backwards

With most things, if you start by thinking about the end of the process and then work backwards, you'll find you are far more successful than if you simply start at the beginning and hope for the best. It's obvious with cooking, for example. You start creating a delicious meal knowing what you want it to look and taste like. You visualise the end result and that determines what ingredients you buy and how you cook, and later present, them. Or take the story of the three little pigs. Only one of the little pigs realised that he was building a house in order to keep the wolf out. He started by working out the end first – what he wanted that house for. The other two little pigs hadn't bothered to think about the real reason they wanted their homes.

Do you know what you really want people to be saying about you and your life when you die? What is really important to you in your life? Do you know what your goals are? Or have you just been carrying on with what you do because it's the easiest option?

If you think of your funeral, imagine what you would like to have said about you by four key speakers: a member of your family, a friend, a colleague and someone from your local community. Think of the eulogies you'd like to hear and use them to start planning your life – knowing what you want the end result to be will help you work out just how to get there.

Never Again

Every now and then knowing what you don't want can help you move forward in unexpected ways. Although your intuition already knows what you never want to do again, sometimes expressing it and taking action can feel daunting. You might know intuitively if you're working with the wrong person, but until you get asked what you never want to do again, you might not consciously express that feeling. When you are asked, you may well find that without a moment's hesitation you'll write 'I never want to work with my business partner again'. Making thought conscious means you can begin moving into your new life without a backwards glance – and without your business partner.

Draw up a list of at least 5 things you never want to do again. Answer this question without thinking too much about it – just pretend to be that 5-year-old child going 'I hate …', and you may find you know exactly what it is that you never want to do again. If you want your list to be longer, just carry on.

1. ....

2. ....

3. ....

4. ....

5. ....

My Visual Future

Collect masses of colour magazines and tear out any pictures of your future – how you would like it to be. It could be anything: a state-of-the-art loft space; an easel and some paints; a good-looking member of the opposite sex; a tool kit; a huge office space; a smiling family; a tiny cottage in the middle of nowhere plus sheepdog; a circus troupe – or all of them. It is entirely up to you. Make the collage below or on a sheet of large paper. Cover it with these pictures of your new life.

'If you don't have a dream, how are you going to make a dream come true?'

Oscar Hammerstein

Finding Your Passion

Your Life Goal is defined by your heart – by what you want. It is what will inspire you daily, keep you focused and help you make decisions on everything. By now you may know intuitively what you want your Life Goal to be. It is what you passionately want to do – something you want to achieve in the future – possibly over the next five years or so. It may be that you want to travel the world, or start your own business, or it may be something vaguer, like to become happy and settled. If you haven't yet decided what your Life Goal is, look at your Balance Chart for inspiration.

Commit yourself. Write down your Life Goal here and date it :

....

....

....

Bite-size chunks

Although your Life Goal is probably emotion-led, you now want your brain to work out how you're going to achieve it. The weekly 'short-term' goals that you are already setting yourself are the tools that will help you achieve your Life Goal. You can see in football how a 'Life Goal', such as 'wanting to win the cup' can easily be broken down – firstly, working backwards, into long-term goals (winning each match to qualify for the next one), and then into short-term daily or weekly goals (such as work-outs, learning new techniques etc). The football Life Goal is time-based and quantifiable and that's how your Life Goal will be broken down too.

Even if your Life Goal is to be happy – something that seems totally passion-driven – you can break it down into measurable parts.

Breaking Down Your Future

If you break down your Life Goal into long-term goals, it's easier to discover how to get what you want for your future.

Life Goal	Long-term goals	Short term goals
eg win cup	win each match	buy new boots
		train daily
		learn new ball skills
eg be settled and happy	lose weight	no biscuits
	feel more confident	get haircut
	new home, find new job,	go to estate agent
	new partner	visit clubs
	etc	
eg save the planet	make home greener	buy re-cycling bin
	join political party	read manifestoes
	find a charity I can help	look on internet
	encourage awareness	write to MP
	etc	

Deciding On Long-Term Goals

Set yourself deadlines as to when you want to achieve your long-term goals by.

To do this, it may help you to think in terms of 'Where do I want to be in 3 months, 6 months, 1 year and 5 years?'

Where I want to be in:

3 months: ....

6 months: ....

1 year: ....

5 years: ....

Working with the above information, write down

My long-term goals	When I want to achieve them by

Making Your Goals Measurable

'I want to lose weight' is most definitely a goal, but if you give it a specific reason – eg 'When I lose 3 centimetres around my hips I can wear my favourite jeans again' – you've suddenly got a measurable long-term goal (you want to lose 3 centimetres), and a real reason to lose that weight (you want to get into those jeans). If you can also give yourself a deadline, such as 'I want to be wearing those jeans for a party in 3 months time', you'll be able to tell whether you've achieved your goal or not.

Mental Acrobatics

For greater incentive, write down each of your long-term goals (and your Life Goal) in the present tense – as if you had already achieved them. If instead of writing 'I want to lose weight', you write 'Now that I'm thinner I look great in my jeans', you'll begin to feel as if achieving your goal is possible.

Here are a few examples.

long-term goal	write down (for example)
eg feeling confident	I enjoy parties and meeting new people
	I no longer worry about giving a presentation
eg new home	my new home is so big I can invite my friends round
	I want to stay in this home forever
eg new job	I have a rewarding job and I am praised by my boss
	my working hours suit my lifestyle much better
eg new relationship	I love sharing my evenings with my new partner
	my new partner makes me laugh

Write your long-term goals down as if you'd already achieved them.

....

....

Goals You Can Achieve

Once you have decided on your long-term goals, break them down again into short-term goals. You won't be able to achieve all these short-term goals at the same time so stagger them and do one or two a week.

For example, take the weight loss long-term goal. You may decide to go to a group for support, so :

Short-term goal for Week 1 : find your nearest group
Short-term goal for Week 2 : persuade a friend to come with you
Short-term goal for Week 3 : go to the first meeting

Set relaxed and realistic time frames or you may feel overwhelmed and even despondent if things don't happen as quickly as you predicted. Give yourself time between starting long-term goals. Be kind to yourself.

Making a Time Chart

Making a time chart will help you decide what you're going to do each week (turn over to see what your time chart might look like).

Keep Re-evaluating

You may achieve goals more quickly than you thought you would or become more confident and decide to set a more ambitious Life Goal for yourself. Keep checking your Life Goal to make sure it's still what you want.

Can you measure your results?

No matter how vague your goal is, set short-term goals that are measurable. If your goal is finding a new partner, for example, take small steps forward. For example, 'I want to talk to one new person a week who is eligible' or 'I want to interview a dating agency a week'.

Be positive about your goals

Look forward to your goals. They are goals that you want to achieve – you're doing them for you. Think about how you'll feel when you've done them.

A Sample Time Chart (for 6 months)

Week

	1	2	3	4	5	6	7	8	9	10
Life Goal: To feel settled and happy										
Long-term goal: I'm in my own home										
Walk streets to find a location I like	✓	✓	✓				✓			
Search internet				✓						
Visit estate agents										
etc.										
Long-term goal: I have a rewarding job										
List my skills				✓	✓					
Ask a friend to review and add to						✓		✓		
Write cv									✓	✓
Go to an agency										
etc.										
Long-term goal: I look great										
Ask a friend to help decide on a new look										
Visit a personal shopper										
Get a hair cut										
etc.										
Long-term goal: I weigh 60 kilos										
Find the nearest support group			✓							
Ask a friend to come too				✓						
Go to meetings						✓	✓	✓	✓	✓
etc.										
Long-term goal: I have a new partner										
Ask couples how they met	✓									
Invite friends round							✓			✓
Visit club										
etc.										

Week

11	12	13	14	15	16	17	18	19	20	21	22	23	24	25	26
✓					✓		✓		✓	✓			✓	✓	
				✓				✓	✓						
	✓	✓	✓												
✓	✓	✓	✓	✓	✓	✓	✓	✓	✓	✓	✓	✓	✓	✓	✓
						✓		✓			✓	✓			✓

My Time Chart (for 6 months)

Week

	1	2	3	4	5	6	7	8	9	10

Life Goal:

Long-term goal:

Long-term goal:

Long-term goal:

Long-term goal:

Long-term goal:

Week

11	12	13	14	15	16	17	18	19	20	21	22	23	24	25	26

Being Positive

When working on your goal, think positively. Be honest and realistic about who you are and about what negative thoughts you may put in the place of achieving your goal. The more honest you are about these negative thoughts, the more easily you're going to be able to do the next bit which is to find your way out of them. For example:

Negative thoughts	New Positive thoughts (think them in the present tense as if you are doing them)
I'm OK really	I'm inspired to change
What if I fail?	What's the worst that could happen?
I'm such a perfectionist	I'm doing it perfectly
I can't get a job with no qualifications	I'm getting qualified
I'm too old to change	I can do anything I want to
Diets don't work for me	I've found a diet I can stick to
I'm too busy to sort out my wardrobe	I'm decluttering 10 minutes a day
My relationships always go wrong	This time it's different
Where do I meet new people?	I'm asking my friends how to
I can't afford a new place	I'm going to talk to an estate agent

Write down your negative thoughts with their new, positive echoes

My negative thoughts	My new positive thoughts (written in the present tense)
....	....
....	....
....	....

Future Me is about …

accessing my talents
inspiring myself
deciding on my future
being aware of my days
enjoying my days
am I missing anything?
planning ahead
imagining my future
deciding on my future
planning my future
positive thinking
breaking down my goal

3

moving **forward**

Your Balance Chart

Once you've decided what you want from your life, it's time to get on with achieving it. This chapter will get you going.

Before reading about how to move forwards, complete and date this Balance Chart and then compare it with your last two. Get curious about the changes you are making in your life.

what am I waiting for?

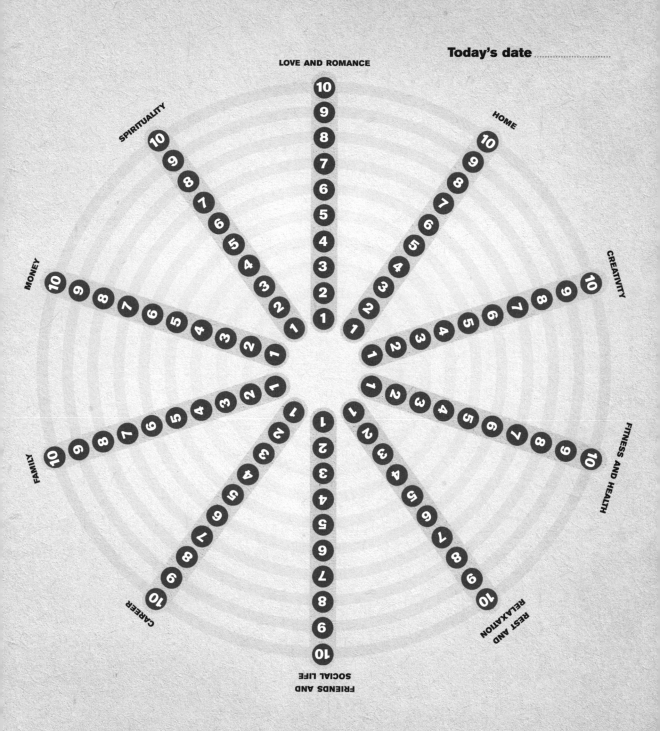

Today's date ....

'Each indecision brings its own delays and days are lost lamenting over lost days. Are you in earnest? Seize this very minute; whatever you can do or dream you can do, begin it. For boldness has magic, power, and genius in it. Begin it now.'

Johann Wolfgang von Goethe

The Power of Focusing

Moving forward is about having something to move forward to. In the previous chapter you set yourself a goal and broke it down into manageable chunks. You know what you want to achieve. This chapter is about managing your time and overcoming obstacles so that you can get to where you want to be as quickly and efficiently as possible.

No matter how determined you are, there will be times in any day when you may feel unfocused about what you want to do. The moment you have more than one option, you feel confused.

You work best when you focus on one thing at a time. If you have too many options it often helps just to grab one and do it. It doesn't matter which option it is, because the act of doing something will give you a sense of satisfaction and control and other decisions will fall naturally into place.

Your Big Picture

On this page stick a picture of where you would like to be in five or ten years – your end goal. If you are starting a business, for example, you may want to put a picture of the golden arches here or another business that you aspire to – or an entrepreneur whom you admire. Just stick any picture you want to on top of the bull's eye below. If you are retraining as a vet, for example, you may want to put a picture of yourself with an animal here. This page will be something to inspire you – a big picture of your future.

   When you're feeling unfocused, turn to your big picture and it will instantly re-focus you. You'll know what you want to do with your time.

Making Time For Your New Life

Most of us are always rushing around and making excuses for why we aren't getting on with what we want to do – let alone making time to change our lives. And yet they say that if you want something done, ask a busy person to do it.

Busy people are organised and efficient – they get things done. In order to move forward, you too have to manage your day well so that you get a feeling of satisfaction at the end of it, plus some time to think about your new life. Because once you're in control of your time you can start thinking what you want from it.

There is a very simple life coaching illustration that will help you to start taking responsibility for your time.

The Jam Jar Illustration

Imagine a jam jar into which you put three large stones. It seems quite full. Now tip in as many pebbles as you can. Watch them go into all the cracks. Is the jar full now? Not quite. Pour in some sand. That will seep in between the pebbles. The jar must be full now. No it's not. Pour in some water until the water reaches the brim. Your jam jar is now full.

Now try doing it the other way round. Put in the same amount of water, then sand, then pebbles. Now try putting in the stones – they won't fit. They'll stick out at the top, resting on the pebbles and sand which have sunk to the bottom.

This is a metaphor for your life:
The jam jar = your day
The stones = your priorities/goals – the things that will move you forward in your life
The pebbles = fixed commitments (work, committee meetings, evening classes)
The sand = other major chores you have to do (commuting, food shopping, school runs)
The water = never ending little tasks (replying to e-mails, paying bills, tidying up)

Some of our days can appear full of water or sand (waiting for the plumber, the phone always ringing etc.) It's difficult to fit the stones in and feels frustrating. You can't move forward.

Take control. Every day, first schedule in your goals (the stones) so your other priorities (the pebbles, sand and water) have to fit around them. That way, even if you have a day that appears full of water (niggly tasks), you can work out an appropriate stone (goal) for it. For example, instead of being annoyed that you have to stay in all day and wait for the plumber, think of a stone you can do at home while you're waiting for him/her. Or make mending the blocked drain one of your stones, then you won't mind waiting.

Your stones are the future of your life – so find time for them first.

3 stones are about right for a day – you could choose:

- **one for your career**
- **one for the area on the balance chart on which you had a low score**
- **one for you – a treat (eg time to be spontaneous)**

Each stone is a very small chunk – the very next thing that you want to do on your project or towards your goal. It's a manageable piece of your goal. Once it is done you break off another chunk (your next stone) and so on, until the goal is completed. Make each chunk small so you can achieve it and give yourself a feeling of satisfaction.

And, if you don't achieve your stone that day – do it the next.

'Derive happiness in oneself from a good day's work, from illuminating the fog that surrounds us.'

Henri Matisse

Focusing On Your Stones

Decide on one or more things that you'd like to achieve next week. If they need breaking down into manageable tasks ('stones'), do that – or make each of them a stone. Then, think about how you are going to make time to do them – might you have to give something up (television, chatting on the phone, computer games etc)?

What do I want to achieve?

Put your stones for the week into the appropriate day – and then do them.

Day 1   (fill in date) ....

Stone 1 ....

Stone 2 ....

Stone 3 ....

Day 2   (fill in date) ....

Stone 1 ....

Stone 2 ....

Stone 3 ....

Day 3   (fill in date) ....

Stone 1 ....

Stone 2 ....

Stone 3 ....

Day 4   (fill in date) ....

Stone 1 ....

Stone 2 ....

Stone 3 ....

Day 5   (fill in date) ....

Stone 1 ....

Stone 2 ....

Stone 3 ....

Day 6   (fill in date) ....

Stone 1 ....

Stone 2 ....

Stone 3 ....

Day 7   (fill in date) ....

Stone 1 ....

Stone 2 ....

Stone 3 ....

Maximising Your Time

Once you're in control of your time, you're in control of your life. As well as setting goals, become aware of yourself and how you perform during the day so you can play to your strengths.

5 Ways to Maximise your Time

● Schedule in most of your tasks at the time of day you're at your best. That may be any time during the day – get curious about how you function.

● Build in a little time every day to set your 'stones' (short-term goals) and organise the next day. Last thing at night or first thing in the morning are often good times.

● Prioritise everything – including your goals. You can only focus on one task at a time, so pick the most important one first.

● Learn how to re-focus. So that when you're interrupted, you can get back to where you were as quickly as possible – remember your big picture (page 90).

● Never put off until tomorrow what you can do today. If in doubt, do. It will free up your mind and enable you to cross something off your list.

Dealing with the 5 Major Time Wasters

1 **Interruptions & emergencies**

● Be flexible

● Plan for 50% of your time – allow 50% for the unexpected

● Schedule routine work for when you expect to be interrupted

● If you are interrupted, help yourself to focus again by calmly asking yourself, 'What is the most important thing I can be doing with my time right now?' Then do it.

● If you really don't want to be interrupted :
    Put phones on answer phone
    Don't answer the door
    Ignore e-mails

2 **Cluttered routines**

- Often we think we're the only people who can do things, but we're not. Delegate anything you can. Work on what only you can do. Simplify your day

3 **Procrastination**

- We are all capable of procrastination. If you can – just do it. That's being effective. Don't worry if what you're doing is perfect or not, just go for it
- A legitimate procrastination is if you're not in the mood to do something you're dreading, like make that important phone call. Instead do something that you know will make you feel good. That sense of accomplishment will make you feel empowered and will get you in the mood for that phone call

4 **Can't say 'No'**

- Once you are convinced of your goal and the importance of your priorities, you'll find it much easier to say 'No'
- Practice makes perfect. Say 'No' to small things and your confidence will grow

5 **Waiting for other people**

- Keep low priority tasks to do while waiting
- Telephone business colleagues or clients first to double check they are coming as agreed
- Ask a neighbour or neighbouring business if they can take in the delivery you are expecting or let the plumber in so that you don't have to wait at home all day
- Tell friends who are always late to come half an hour earlier than you want them

Setting Priorities

Looking at your Balance Chart will give you an instant indication of whether you are living life according to your priorities. Just see how different your 'to do' list might look if you prioritised it.

First write a rough 'to do' list of everything you have to do this week.

My 'to do' list

....

....

....

....

Now write out your list again according to your goal/s

My 'to do' list prioritised to help me achieve my goals

1 ....   10 ....

2 ....   11 ....

3 ....   12 ....

4 ....   13 ....

5 ....   14 ....

6 ....   15 ....

7 ....   16 ....

8 ....   17 ....

9 ....   18 ....

'Imagination is more important than knowledge. Knowledge is limited, but imagination encircles the world.'

Oscar Hammerstein

Using Positive Visualisation

As well as managing your time, you now want to *empower* yourself to achieve your goal. One way not only to give yourself confidence, but also to clarify your goals and how you are going to achieve them is positive visualisation. You will use your mind to become the person you want to be.

The premise of positive visualisation is that if you can see or express your goal you can reach it. It is based on the principle that your mind and your body are intimately connected. By visualising or describing your goal in minute detail you are actually imagining your future and planning the route to get there. You may feel positive visualisation sounds far-fetched, yet we all use negative visualisation by imagining worst case scenarios. In positive visualisation, by directing your daydreams, you programme your subconscious to expect those good things you have just fantasised about.

As children we used to use positive visualisations automatically to fantasise about winning the race at sports day or acting brilliantly in the school play. Now we can use them consciously for moving forward.

There are two parts to Positive Visualisation :

1. **Visualisation:** The image (or words, thoughts, sensations) about what you want to happen. Make your visualisation as clear, vivid and detailed as possible. For example, if you want to become financially solvent you might imagine standing at the bank and paying in lots of cheques. Visualise this in colour, listen to what you and the cashier are saying, notice the texture of the crisp cheques, smell the smell of money and become aware of how you are feeling.

2. **Positive:** focusing on solutions. Using the above bank scenario, think about how to achieve it. Where are the cheques coming from? How did you get them? What has to happen?

There are two ways of using visualisation:

1. Process Visualisation – visualising the process you have to go through to achieve the goal you want

You may imagine yourself getting into the yoga position you want to achieve, or giving an inspirational speech or cooking a wonderful meal. The way Process Visualisation works is that by continually repeating (or mentally rehearsing) what you want to do, you acquire a kind of 'memory' of a successful action and at the same time condition the subconscious mind with the outcome you expect to achieve.

2. Result Visualisation – creating mental pictures of the goal or result as if it has already happened

The yoga position has been successfully completed. You are doing it. You feel that inner glow of confidence; you imagine what the room looks like at that moment. You notice who else is there, what you are wearing and what it feels like. Or, you are now a lecturer giving regular speeches and being congratulated on your most recent talk or you are sitting back contentedly with your friends having just enjoyed one of your delicious meals.

By doing result visualisation you will be making many decisions about what you want from your future and, without consciously thinking about it too much, planning in quite minute detail how to get there.

Keep visualising

- Visualise about one goal at a time
- Each time you catch yourself thinking negatively remind yourself that that is your old way of thinking and replace that old pattern with your new, positive visualisation
- Feel positive when you visualise. Focus on your visualisation with total commitment and conviction. Visualise several times a day
- If you prefer words, thoughts or sensations, use them instead of or as well as images

Imagining Your Future

Look at your Balance Chart and find an area you would like to work on. It could be the area of your goal or the area you scored the lowest in or another area that seems more pressing at the moment. You can choose two areas to visualise about if you want to.

Area 1 (eg to be in a loving relationship)

Area 2

In your ideal life, in your wildest fantasy, what would those parts of your life look like in 6 months? In 1 year? In 5 years?

Area 1
in 6 months (eg having met someone I'm attracted to)

in 1 year (eg moving in together)

in 5 years (eg having a child with them)

Area 2
in 6 months

In 1 year

5 years

When are you going to start practising positive visualisation?

To experience a visualisation of your future, log on to our website (www.affordablelifecoaching.org).

Positive Affirmations

Positive affirmations are positive (and realistic) thoughts or statements that you repeat to yourself at various times during the day. Positive affirmations will also boost your confidence and help you bring into your life the things you want. As you talk to yourself all day, and therefore can influence yourself more than anyone else can, so you can also move yourself forward more than anyone else can.

Why Positive Affirmations?

Positive Affirmations are your new way of thinking. You use them to counteract any negative affirmations, such as 'I've always been hopeless at maths' or 'I always get this wrong', that you can be so good at using.

How do positive affirmations work?

By repeating them you impress the subconscious mind to guide your thoughts and actions into a positive direction

Using positive affirmations effectively

- Choose a maximum of 3 positive affirmations at any one time (eg personal, business, health)
- Focus on one desired outcome for each affirmation
- Write each positive affirmation in the present tense (as if they were happening) and in the first person (eg 'I am beautiful', 'I attract all the money I want', 'I am a natural entrepreneur', 'I am confident'.)
- Keep positive affirmations short, and avoid negative expressions (eg say 'I am the perfect shape and feel great' rather than 'I am no longer fat')
- Repeat each one several times a day
- Act as if they are already working and yielding positive results
- Infuse positive affirmations with total commitment and conviction
- Each time you go back to thinking negatively, catch yourself and gently remind yourself that that is your old way of thinking
- For extra effect, use the affirmations with positive visualisation

By changing your mindset from negative to positive you are giving yourself permission to grow, to change and to take risks – to create a better life for yourself.

Conscious Fear

Although you can use both positive visualisation and affirmations to move yourself forward, unless you overcome your fears you will stay stuck. Ironically it's easier to try new things than to be constantly fearful. By trying new things, you begin to realise you can tackle anything. You become brave, whereas if you're feeling fearful about your future, you will be unable to think clearly, you'll feel underconfident and unwilling to take risks. You may even get gloomy and despondent.

We all feel fear, especially when it comes to change. Fear is a product of your mind, but it's at the root of everything that keeps you small and holds you back. Be conscious about your fear and do what you fear anyway. Imagine that there is no choice. Turn your fear into excitement and let it propel you forwards. Failure isn't failing at what you attempt to do – failing is not attempting at all.

5 things to do when you feel frightened

1   Be conscious of your fear. Say 'I'm scared'
2   Analyse what it is you're really afraid of
3   Write down how you're feeling – it looks less frightening written down
4   Tackle fears when they are small rather than overwhelming
5   See if there's anything practical you can do to overcome your fear

6 tools for conquering fear

1   **Positive affirmations** (such as 'I'm great at this')
2   **Negative visualisation** (imagine the worst that could happen)
3   **Positive visualisation** (imagine the positive outcome you want)
4   **Focus on solutions** (see each problem as a learning tool – 'that didn't work so what can I do instead'?)
5   **Think of the alternatives** (are there any?)
6   **Choose role models** (if they can do it, you can too)

Best Case Scenarios

Make a list of all your previous fears about the future (put down anything – how frightened you were about the boat trip you were going on; how worried you were that your friends weren't going to get on with each other; how convinced you were that your speech was going to be a disaster etc).

Previous fears	Were they justified?

How many of those fears were justified? Cross out each of those fears that turned out OK in the end.

   With the fears you have left (the fears you were justified in having), see if you can understand why you were justified in having them. Were they about things you weren't meant to be doing? Was there actually a silver lining under each of those 'clouds'?

Trust that everything happens for the best.

'Failure is the only opportunity to more intelligently begin again.'

Henry Ford

Getting Motivated

Even if you feel inspired by your goal, there are times when achieving it feels like very hard work, and it's times like those when it's helpful if you know what motivates you. In the past you've achieved the things you wanted to achieve – or at least most of them. It's easy to downplay that list of achievements by saying you 'enjoyed' doing all those things, but enjoyment can be a key motivational tool.

If you want to change your life and your resolve stops and you're not moving forward any longer, it may be that you haven't understood what keeps you motivated. Each of us has different motivational tools, right now you're going to get curious about what motivates you.

Deadlines
You may want deadlines and love to do everything at the last minute or you may prefer to pace yourself.
Fear
For some the fear of things getting worse can be a strong motivator.
Acting as if
Being your own role model can help you radiate self-belief and lift you out of yourself and into a more powerful frame of mind.
Getting energised
Do whatever it takes to wake you up and get you moving forward – music, walking, exercising, dancing.
Rewards
Rewards can be useful – 'If you make that phone call you're dreading, you can phone a friend afterwards.'
Praise/appreciation
Works like a reward – can be a hug from a friend, a 'Well done' from a colleague or a 'Thanks, Mum' from a child.
Accountability
Accountability is when you don't want to let yourself (or another) down. You feel you have a responsibility to do what you said you were going to do.

Making a plan

Making a plan may help you focus on what you want. The plan can be as small as you want it to be, or a large, time-tabled projection.

Positive affirmations

The more resistance you have when you first use each positive affirmation, the more you may find that those are the ones that will be the most effective.

Competition

Competition works for many – from athletes to barristers.

Inspiration

Looking at beautiful things or watching others overcome incredible obstacles can be very inspiring. Become an inspiration to yourself.

Passion

The emotional energy that gave you your goal can also motivate you to continue with it.

The consequences of not taking action

Imagine a worst case scenario: 'If I did nothing – what might happen?'

Being depended on

Some hate being depended on, but you may find that having to do something for someone else works for you.

Working in a team

Does working as part of a team motivate you or do you just like to consult others as and when you want to?

Listening to your heart

Your intuition will know if you are doing the right thing and will assist you with each step on the way towards your dream.

Believing you are lucky

If you believe you are lucky, you know that you are being looked after and that everything happens for the best.

Motivation is what's going to keep you on track and make your dream happen. Know *why* you want to achieve something and what inspires you. Trusting that you can achieve your dream and feeling that you want to – that's motivation.

Your motivational tools

Give each of these motivational tools a mark between 1-10 as to how effective they are at motivating you. Add any of your own if you want to.

Deadlines	....	Fear	....
Acting as if	....	Getting energised	....
Rewards	....	Praise/appreciation	....
Accountability	....	Making a plan	....
Positive Affirmations	....	Competition	....
Inspiration	....	Passion	....
Consequences of not taking action	....	Being depended on	....
Working in a team	....	Listening to your heart	....
Believing you are lucky	....	Enjoyment	....

Write down as many things as you can think of that you've completed and work out what motivated you to complete them.

I completed
(eg writing this book)

what motivated me?
(eg passion/ enjoyment/ rewards/ desire to be helpful)

....

....

....

....

....

....

Moving Forward is all about ...

questioning why I'm waiting

making the most of my time

deciding on my priorities

visualising and affirming

working with my future

conquering fear

deciding what motivates me

assembling my motivational tools

the power of me

4

the power of me

Your Balance Chart

You're already moving forward into your new life. This chapter will make sure you've got all your energy behind you.

Before finding out how to access your power, complete and date this Balance Chart. Compare this chart with your last few and notice the changes. If some areas have got lower values than before, it isn't necessarily cause for despondency. It may mean you are focusing on the areas you want to.

how am I feeling today?

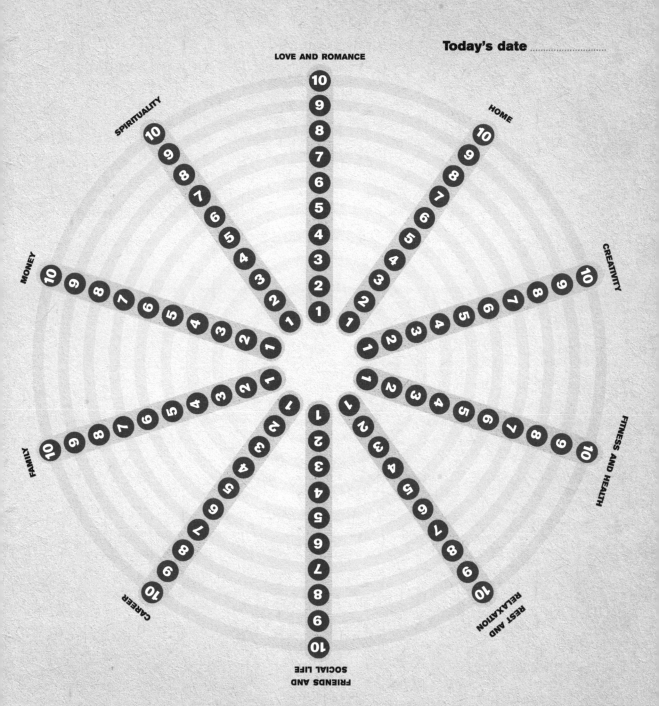

Getting The Life Balance You Want

Feeling powerful is about balancing your life so it's the way you want it. Every time you fill in a Balance Chart it gives you a snapshot of where you are in your life and helps you see whether where you are is congruent with your needs and priorities.

You're not aiming for a perfect circle because there's no such thing as an ideal balance that would suit us all. Each of us aiming for a '10' in every aspect of our Balance Chart would imply we were all the same, but we're not. We all want a different life balance depending on our ages, our personalities, our energy levels and our time of life. There is an ideal balance for you at this moment of your life depending on your goals and priorities.

If you have a lop-sided Balance Chart, it may mean you are :

- in love
- over-worked
- a teenager in bed all day
- on a fitness kick

There are 4 ways to find your ideal life balance

1. Recognise that your life balance is to do with your priorities
2. Understand that what suits you now may not suit you later
3. Be aware that we are all different and that we all change
4. Balance your life according to your goals

You can find it difficult to achieve your ideal life balance because of 'stuff' – unfulfilled tasks, 'to do' lists, other people's pressures and ultimately your own pressure. Regaining power and achieving your ideal life is to do with moving from passive to active living.

Passive living	Active living
caught in a time squeeze	time for everything important
never enough minutes in the day	relaxed
stressed	positive about your future
out of control	in control

'The best and safest thing is to keep a balance in your life, acknowledge the great powers around us and in us. If you can do that, and live that way, you are really a wise man.'

Euripides

It's Your Time

Taking control of your time is moving from passive to active living. Once your day is structured the way you want it to be, it will be long enough to fit everything you want to do into it. So, what are you waiting for? Make time for you.

Dead-head your life regularly even though it may be difficult. Look through your routines and see which you could prune. Do you want a different structure around your life now you are changing? Do you want different people around you? Do you want a new routine?

1. **Build a routine – make time for everything you want to do**
- Decide on a fixed time to pay bills and do paperwork
- Plan short regular slots for household chores
- Book in 'special time' for you to relax and to spend time with your family and partners
- Organise enjoyable treats for the weekend in advance – or indecision can take over

2. **Get support/delegate**
- At work – find it if you can
- At home – from your family, and involve children and neighbours

3. **Adopt time-savers/multi-task**
- Files for favourite recipes
- Cook occasional meals in advance
- Lists of emergency telephone numbers
- Files for directions to other people's homes kept in the car

4. **Cut down on time-thieves such as**
- Other people and their agendas
- Telephones – especially mobiles
- E-mails
- Television
- Computers in general – including games

You Decide

By becoming aware of what you spend your time on you'll be able to take control of those minutes in the future.

Keep a diary for a week. Imagine you were charging out each half-hour of your day, so record it accurately. This diary will let you know if you're in control of your life – if you're spending time on the things you want to spend time on.

Once you've filled in your diary you'll be able to see if it fits with your goals :

- Is there as much time for your partner as you wanted there to be?
- Did you send out all your invoices/pay your bills?
- Did you see your parents this week?
- Did you exercise as much as you wanted to?
- Did you manage to have that trip to the cinema?
- Did you complete your project?
- Did you have time to meditate?

am I doing what I want?

My Life Balance Diary

Date ....

6.00	14.00 ....
6.30	14.30 ....
7.00	15.00 ....
7.30	15.30 ....
8.00	16.00 ....
8.30	16.30 ....
9.00	17.00 ....
9.30	17.30 ....
10.00	18.00 ....
10.30	18.30 ....
11.00	19.00 ....
11.30	19.30 ....
12.00	20.00 ....
12.30	20.30 ....
13.00	21.00 ....
13.30	21.30 ....

My Life Balance Diary

Date ....

6.00	14.00 ....
6.30	14.30 ....
7.00	15.00 ....
7.30	15.30 ....
8.00	16.00 ....
8.30	16.30 ....
9.00	17.00 ....
9.30	17.30 ....
10.00	18.00 ....
10.30	18.30 ....
11.00	19.00 ....
11.30	19.30 ....
12.00	20.00 ....
12.30	20.30 ....
13.00	21.00 ....
13.30	21.30 ....

am I wasting my time?

My Life Balance Diary

Date ....

6.00	14.00 ....
6.30	14.30 ....
7.00	15.00 ....
7.30	15.30 ....
8.00	16.00 ....
8.30	16.30 ....
9.00	17.00 ....
9.30	17.30 ....
10.00	18.00 ....
10.30	18.30 ....
11.00	19.00 ....
11.30	19.30 ....
12.00	20.00 ....
12.30	20.30 ....
13.00	21.00 ....
13.30	21.30 ....

My Life Balance Diary   Date ....

6.00	**14.00** ....
6.30	**14.30** ....
7.00	**15.00** ....
7.30	**15.30** ....
8.00	**16.00** ....
8.30	**16.30** ....
9.00	**17.00** ....
9.30	**17.30** ....
10.00	**18.00** ....
10.30	**18.30** ....
11.00	**19.00** ....
11.30	**19.30** ....
12.00	**20.00** ....
12.30	**20.30** ....
13.00	**21.00** ....
13.30	**21.30** ....

am I becoming more efficient?

My Life Balance Diary

Date ....

6.00	14.00 ....
6.30	14.30 ....
7.00	15.00 ....
7.30	15.30 ....
8.00	16.00 ....
8.30	16.30 ....
9.00	17.00 ....
9.30	17.30 ....
10.00	18.00 ....
10.30	18.30 ....
11.00	19.00 ....
11.30	19.30 ....
12.00	20.00 ....
12.30	20.30 ....
13.00	21.00 ....
13.30	21.30 ....

My Life Balance Diary

Date ....

6.00	14.00 ....
6.30	14.30 ....
7.00	15.00 ....
7.30	15.30 ....
8.00	16.00 ....
8.30	16.30 ....
9.00	17.00 ....
9.30	17.30 ....
10.00	18.00 ....
10.30	18.30 ....
11.00	19.00 ....
11.30	19.30 ....
12.00	20.00 ....
12.30	20.30 ....
13.00	21.00 ....
13.30	21.30 ....

is there time for me now?

My Life Balance Diary

Date ....

6.00	....	**14.00**	....
6.30	....	**14.30**	....
7.00	....	**15.00**	....
7.30	....	**15.30**	....
8.00	....	**16.00**	....
8.30	....	**16.30**	....
9.00	....	**17.00**	....
9.30	....	**17.30**	....
10.00	....	**18.00**	....
10.30	....	**18.30**	....
11.00	....	**19.00**	....
11.30	....	**19.30**	....
12.00	....	**20.00**	....
12.30	....	**20.30**	....
13.00	....	**21.00**	....
13.30	....	**21.30**	....

' Time is the coin of your life. It is the only coin you have, and only you can determine how it will be spent. Be careful lest you let other people spend it for you.'

Carl Sandberg, American Poet

Totally Balanced

When you think about the balance in your life, think of your life as a whole. Not just work/life balance, but duty/play, routine/spontaneity, selfishness/altruism, being awake/sleeping and all the other areas in your life.

Balance ...	with ...
working outdoors ...	improving your mind (studying, reading)
demanding brain work ...	calmness (yoga, knitting)
looking after children ...	doing something for yourself
working alone ...	seeing friends/going to a club
being sad ...	laughter

Now make a list of everything you really want to do but never have time for.

Look back at your diary and think about what you would have to change in your life to make time for those things.

For example – getting up earlier, watching less television, delegating more, saying 'No', dropping a commitment that's past its sell-by date. What can you change now to give yourself more time?

....

....

....

....

....

....

Make Space For The New

As you think about what's missing in your life, it's an ideal time to clear away the debris of the former you and make space for the new you. Decluttering sounds simple, but it is a potent method of change.

Once you begin decluttering, your spirits will be lifted; you'll release a huge amount of positive energy, and experience a much lighter feeling inside. It will soon become a habit that you'll look forward to. Starting a new life means starting a clean slate – letting go of things, people and mental clutter that you no longer want.

Hold on to anything that nourishes you, supports you, is beautiful, uplifting. Get rid of presents you don't like (tactfully), things with no meaning, things 'you may need one day'. Give something up and you'll gain something of greater value in return.

5 reasons why decluttering is so difficult

1. It forces us to make choices
2. It reminds us of unfinished tasks – things we have failed to do
3. It takes time
4. It's tiring
5. It can seem overwhelming

5 hints to making it easier

1. Start slowly – 10 minutes a day or getting rid of 1 item a day
2. Start with a contained task – a small box or cupboard
3. Concentrate on one job at a time
4. Choose to make a change every day
5. Ask a friend to help – next time you can help them

On our website is a visualisation that will inspire you in your decluttering. It will also help you to realise the power of your intuition – you already know what you want to clear. Learn to trust that knowledge.

Plan Of Action

Once you start decluttering, appreciate how much lighter and freer you feel – and keep that feeling. Although you are decluttering physical things, you will find you have cleared a space into which mental, emotional and physical things can fit. Think of something to fill that new, clear space that makes you feel wonderful. It could be taking up a new hobby, spending more time with friends or doing community work. This is an opportunity to start something new in your life.

Every day this week spend a minimum of 10 minutes decluttering your home.
Without thinking, write down which 7 areas you want to start with. Or, spend 7 days decluttering one large area.

1. ....

2. ....

3. ....

4. ....

5. ....

6. ....

7. ....

Decide when you are going to do that 10 minutes of decluttering. If you keep to a regular time you're more likely to remember.

'Nothing is so fatiguing as the eternal hanging on of an uncompleted task.'

William James

That's What I Want

As well as clutter, each of our lives is filled with things we don't want to put up with. They may be little niggles, like the holes in the pockets of your coat which your money drops through. Or they may be larger annoyances like your children always going to bed too late which makes you nag them or your not-so best friend constantly crying on your shoulder. Or they may be even more serious complaints, like you don't like where you live – or your job. Empowering yourself means tackling the problems in your life, rather than ignoring them and hoping they'll go away.

Many of us put up with things that we really don't want to – it takes effort to do something about them and often we can't be bothered. It could be the 'anything for a quiet life' syndrome which we're all guilty of, but it could also be our anxiety about change and our desire not to hurt others. Writing down a list of things you no longer want in your life will set you on the path of change.

Things I no longer want in my life

1..   6. ....

2..   7. ....

3..   8. ....

4..   9. ....

5..   10..

1 thing from my list that I'm going to change now

....

It's Your Choice

Become curious about your language and listen out for every time you say 'should/ought to/need/must/have to'. Why are you using these words? Do you have too many obligations in your life? Is it because you find it difficult to say that you 'want' something? Or is it that you don't know what you want?

If you practise listening to yourself, you'll find this self-knowledge can move you on enormously. You might find that you live your life doing things that, if you think about it, you don't really want to do.

- Are you going on holiday with your family out of guilt or because you want to?
- Are you staying in a relationship because you have invested so much in it or because you want to?
- Are you in your career because you're looking for approval or because you want to be there?
- Do you know what you want?

Start living a life that is true to you. Of course, there are some real 'musts'. You may have families and friends who need you to look after them. These relationships can be fulfilling as well as essential, but set boundaries around them so you have time for your own life – the life you want.

If you really listened to what you wanted, you might find that some of those 'shoulds' aren't as essential as you thought they were. If you let the world know what you want to do, you are giving others a chance to help you. If you honour your intuition and your true desires you may find the path forward easier than you had at first thought it would be.

Listening To Yourself

Make a day (or at least a few hours) free to do what you want in –
things you wouldn't normally allow yourself to do. During this time do
exactly what your intuition tells you to do. You could :

- Read in the bath
- Update your blog
- Have a game of tennis
- Phone your friends and chat for hours
- Go shopping
- Go for a walk in nature
- Lie on the sofa reading
- Listen to really loud music

Do whatever you want (as long as you're not hurting yourself or anyone
else with your behaviour).

How different is that?

Notice the difference between how you are feeling when you are
following your intuition and doing something you want to do and how
you are feeling when you are doing something you 'ought' to do.

Saying 'No'

Part of the reason we do so many things we don't want to do is because we find it difficult, if not impossible, to say 'No'. But would you make your best friend say 'Yes' if they didn't want to do something? Of course not. So why make yourself?

As adults we believe that saying 'No' can cost us a lot, but being unable to say 'No' can actually cost us a lot more.

If you say 'Yes' to someone when you want to say 'No', you will feel resentful from the moment you've said 'Yes' until the moment whatever you've agreed to do is over – and maybe even after that. Saying 'No' isn't simply being unhelpful. You can still make useful suggestions – 'Why not try so-and-so' or 'What other way could you achieve the same result?' Remember that saying 'No' to others is saying 'Yes' to yourself.

Whenever you are asked a question
1. Pause for a moment
2. Listen to your true desires – if you ignore them now, they'll only resurface later.
3. Decide what you want

As you begin to value yourself and know what you want from your life, so you'll find it becomes easier to say 'No'

You must say 'No'
- When you're overworked
- When you're tired and/or stressed

You have a right to say 'No'
- If you feel you're being taken for granted
- When you don't want to do something

It's good to say 'No'
- Because you feel like it
- When you want to do something else
- When you want some time to yourself
- When it's their problem, not yours

When you say 'No', two things happen
- You begin to feel happier and more energetic
- People value you more when you do say 'Yes'

How to say 'No'

1. Identify your feelings

- Remember the decision is entirely up to you. You don't have to say 'No' if you really don't want to. You can say 'Yes'
- Stall – give yourself some time to work out what your feelings are
- If you want more time, say one of these (or something similar)
    'I must look at my diary ...'
    'I'll have to think about that ...'
    'I'll let you know later today ...'
    'Let me check with my partner ...'
- Use the time you have gained to decide what you really want

2. Saying 'No'

- It's easier to keep the commitment to say 'No' if it's the first word you utter.
- Be pleasant, brief and straightforward. Say something like
    'No, I'm afraid I can't',
    'No, it's not convenient'
    'No, not this time'
- Be pleasant, simple and direct
- An excuse isn't necessary to support your stand
- Give a reason only if you feel you have information that the other party could benefit from

3. Body language

- Keep your voice firm and direct
- Look into their eyes as you say 'No'
- Shake your head 'No' as you say 'No'
- Remember it's OK to say 'No'. If 'No' is the answer you want to give, then your answer is honest and authentic

' Say 'Yes' to the seedlings and a giant forest cleaves the sky. Say 'Yes' to the universe and the planets become your neighbours. Say 'Yes' to dreams of love and freedom. It is the password to utopia.'

Brooks Atkinson, American author

Finding Your Feelings

A list of everything I find very difficult to say 'No' to.
eg being asked to babysit

....

....

....

....

....

A list of everything I'd really like to say 'Yes' to.
eg a holiday

....

....

....

....

Now, 'ink' into my diary some things I want to do.
Because we find it difficult to say 'No' we fudge decisions by pencilling in dates we hope we'll have the strength of mind to refuse as they get closer. Now it's time to ink in some dates for you – things you *want* to do. Time disappears. Don't feel selfish about doing what you want – it is your time.

The Power of Me is all about ...

working out my ideal life
   balance
checking if I'm wasting time
becoming more efficient
making time for me
balanced living
making room for my new life
knowing what I want
listening out for what I want
learning to say 'no' to others
learning to say 'yes' to me

loving me

5

loving me

Your Balance Chart

You've taken control of your life and are moving forward. Now it's time to reflect on what a wonderful person you are.

Before beginning the next chapter about loving yourself, complete and date this Balance Chart and compare it with your last few.

how am I changing?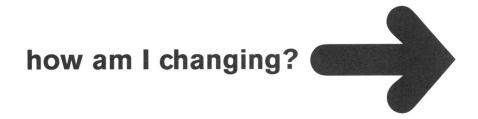

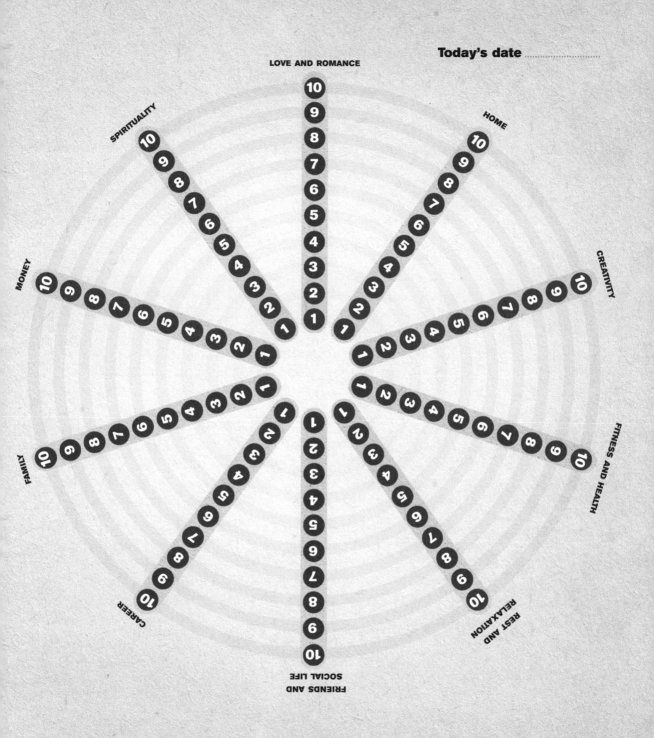

Today's date ....

Unconditional Love

Try to remember the tiny child you were at three and four – how you stuck up for yourself, said 'No' when you didn't want to do something, cried and asked for attention when you needed it, told others what you wanted. In those days you put yourself first – do so again now!

Every day you make compromises. You extend yourself to others even if you're running on empty. If only you were as loving to yourself as you are to others. If only you accepted and forgave yourself as you do others. If only you stopped giving yourself such a tough time.

Why is it so impossible, or even terrifying to love ourselves, to completely accept ourselves? To at least treat ourselves as well as we would our best friend. Do most of us feel so unlovable?

Oscar Wilde once said, 'To love oneself is the beginning of a life-long romance' and it is true. Once you truly love yourself, you'll always be there for yourself. Who else but you will never let you down, never fail you, and always love you passionately.

Think of the relationship you have with your best friends and how wonderful you are to them. Why not give yourself the same treatment?

You'd like …	rather than …
compliments …	self criticism
a few treats …	always looking out for others
looking after …	allowing yourself to be compromised
backing up …	saying 'Yes' to things you don't want to do
enjoying who you are …	trying to fit in

Loving yourself unconditionally doesn't mean dropping your friends. It means treating yourself as one of them. Try it.

You Are Special

Very quickly and unselfconsciously, write down as many things as you can below. Aim for at least five qualities for each question.

What do other people like about you?

Remember what others have said about you. If you don't remember, ask them. Listen carefully and jot it down here before you forget.

1 ....

2 ....

3 ....

4 ....

5 ....

What do you like about yourself?

1 ....

2 ....

3 ....

4 ....

5 ....

It may be difficult for you to blow your own trumpet and write down how wonderful you are. Just do it without thinking. Think about all the things you like about yourself – everything. Go on… admit you're great – you don't have to show anyone what you've written.

Loving Yourself

Self-love is not advocating selfish behaviour and just focusing on yourself. Self-love is about maintaining a balance and caring for yourself as well as others. When you nurture yourself you thrive and have more to give. You are often too busy getting on with your life to look after yourself. If you had a plant and didn't water it, it would die and no longer be able to give pleasure to others. In the same way, only by re-energising yourself will you have the energy for yourself and to share with the people you love and look after.

Many of us are victims of low self-esteem. We sit in cars ignoring our bodies going 'please exercise me', we overeat and rush every meal, we don't go to bed early enough and we don't accomplish everything on our 'to do' list and feel frustrated. Because of all these stresses and strains, we shout at all the people we love the most – especially when they're saying nice things to us. You can see how once you are in the spiral of not loving yourself it affects your entire life – your whole Balance Chart.

Why do so many of us find it difficult to love and take care of ourselves? Why does the cliché 'You can't love anyone else until you can love yourself' make many of us feel so uncomfortable? In our culture we are praised for putting others first. What is known as 'selfish' or 'self-centred' behaviour is a 'bad' thing. But loving yourself isn't selfish. When you feel good about yourself you will feel strong and courageous – you will have deeper resources to draw on and more to give others. Loving yourself will make you comfortable in your own skin and thus happier and warmer towards those you love.

'Self-love, my liege, is not so vile a sin, as self-neglecting.'

William Shakespeare

What Are You Like?

It may help you to think of yourself as a flowering plant or a car that needs to be looked after. Choose a beautiful flower or car that you have comparable qualities to. Are you like a gleaming red Ferrari with tons of energy, bags of flair and always the centre of attention or are you more like a honeysuckle – delicate, sweet-smelling and stretching out to others as far as you can?

What flower or car are you?

....

....

What qualities do you share with this flower or car?
Write down as many as you can.

....

....

....

....

....

....

From now on, remember that the silver Volkswagen you are needs an oil change every now and again or that the striking clematis that is you needs a little water. Look after yourself as well as you would that car or flower.

Making Your Self-Love Grow

There are many ways to make your self-love grow:

Physically

- care for your body: eat nutritiously and exercise regularly
- make sure you're not getting too stressed

Emotionally

- spend time with friends who refresh you
- be of service in the community and to your family (deeper meaning can come into your life through giving to others)

Mentally

- live in the 'now' (be as focused on the present as you can)
- give your brain sustenance (go on courses or to lectures)
- apply yourself to problem solving whenever possible

Spiritually

- meditate, pray or listen to exquisite music
- whenever possible spend a few hours on your own being somewhere beautiful (maybe somewhere from your childhood or somewhere you've recently discovered)

Stop being so hard on yourself. Forgive yourself for anything that's tormenting you from your past. Don't keep telling yourself what you did wrong or what you're doing wrong or what a loser you are. Say, 'OK. I made a mistake. How else am I going to learn? I'll do it better next time'.

Catch yourself when you're about to give yourself another negative message and make it positive. Go one step further. When you do something well, praise yourself and, if you want to, give yourself a healthy treat. In bed every night, go through the previous twelve hours in your mind and think of all the good things you did that day – your achievements.

Take time to tell yourself how wonderful you are. Focus on the potential within you. Live in the now.

'Everybody knows how to raise children, except the people who have them.'

P.J. O'Rourke

Be Who You Are

A feeling of being loved and lovable comes from how we were treated as children. Those lucky enough to have had parents who loved them unconditionally and supported them in everything, will usually have an inner confidence that will help them throughout their life. But those of us whose parents found parenting challenging may have feelings of under-confidence that have stopped us loving ourselves.

Loving yourself is about knowing who you are in your own eyes and not through those of your parents – who, so far, may have been responsible for your self-perception. Your parents, without even meaning to, may have projected their own unresolved issues onto you. It may be that your parents themselves had parents who constantly put them down or criticised them and, instead of working out how they wanted to treat you, they did exactly the same to you – handing down family legacies of put-downs.

These disparaging remarks affect how we are as people, they are our 'learned beliefs'. And, although we may have many 'learned beliefs' from our parents which are supportive and encouraging, most of us, however good our parents were, will have at least some learned beliefs about ourselves which are limiting our potential.

As adults we can begin to distinguish learned beliefs from the truth and realise that the destructive beliefs are often the result of parents who found it difficult to free themselves from their family history. We don't have to be like our parents. We can rid ourselves of these old negative beliefs and move on and discover our true selves.

Live life for yourself. Be who you are, not as your parents saw you. Fulfil your own ambitions, not theirs. Get rid of any unhelpful family legacies before you come to believe them.

changing my learned beliefs

Learned Beliefs

What are at least 5 things I learnt about myself from my mother?

....

....

....

....

....

What are at least 5 things I learnt about myself from my father?

....

....

....

....

They could be things like 'I am artistic' or 'I am a good child', or they could be things like 'I have no imagination' or 'I have two left thumbs and break everything'. (Substitute another authority figure for either parent if you would like to.)

Changing Learned Beliefs

Which of the 'learned beliefs' from my previous list hold me back and which support me.
Write them out again.

Destructive learned beliefs

....

....

....

....

Supportive learned beliefs

....

....

....

....

The beliefs from your past can colour your world of today. Learn to see them as beliefs and not facts. If they don't support you – get rid of them. Cross out the list of destructive beliefs you have written or stick something over it and free yourself to move on.

Growing Up

It's time to grow up. You may have a perfect relationship with your parents, but you may not. You may feel guilty about how rarely you see them, you may blame them for past issues. May be they are still interfering too much in your life or perhaps they've died and you wish you'd known them better.

Growing up means :

- Letting parental ties go so that you are free to grow as a person and live as an independent adult
- Being someone who doesn't want the approval of their parents or anyone else for the way they choose to live their life
- Giving up all blame towards your parents or anyone else for whatever you feel is wrong with your life

You may still harbour childhood grudges and resentments or you may feel guilty that you can't give your parents any more – either practically or emotionally. But all grudges, resentments and guilt do is hold you back and stop you from taking responsibility for your life and making it the life you want. You can't change the past or your parents. Blaming them is pointless – forgive and move on.

1 Choose to be less affected by your parents' demands.
3 Choose to be less affected by your parents putting you down.
4 Decide what you want now out of your relationship with them.
5 Set boundaries about what you will and will not do for them.
6 Focus on knowing what you want now out of the relationship and feel empowered to get it.

Think about your present relationship with regards to your behaviour as well. Is the relationship all your parents' fault or are you partly to blame?

What About You?

Think about yourself now and how you behave. Only answer the questions that are relevant to your current situation.

1 What made your parents behave like that to you?

Do they behave in the same way to other people, such as your brothers and sisters?

....

....

2. What reason have your parents got for thinking that you're always available?

Have you always been available? Do you always make yourself available?

....

....

3. What do you think your parents would say if they were asked why they always put you down?

Or do they put everyone down? Or are you putting yourself down?

....

....

Once you are aware of your role in the family dynamic, you can change. Knowing what you want and setting boundaries will make you happier.

Family Goals

If you have issues with your family, making goals about them will feel good. Use the LIFE Model to see if you don't already know what to do about the current situation with your family. The questions are to stimulate your thinking and awaken your intuition – they are a resource. If you want to, make up questions for yourself that feel more relevant.

LIVING : Analysis of current situation
What is the situation at present with my parents?

....

....

What exactly is causing me problems in my relationship with them (or one of them)?

....

....

Which of these problems is reasonable and which unreasonable? (write the 'reasonable problems' – the ones I can change, down)

....

....

IDEAL : Objectives
Make this a goal I can achieve – remember I can't change my parents. How do I want to improve my relationship with them?

....

....

....

What is a realistic timescale for change?

....

FUEL : Improvement opportunities
How am I going to set about making the changes?

....

....

What (or who) could hinder me and what (or who) could help me?

....

....

What excuses do I always make as to why I don't make these changes?

....

....

ENERGY : Set a date
What am I going to do?

....

....

When am I going to do it?

....

How will I feel when I've done it?

....

....

Trust Yourself

Loving yourself and creating the life you want is all about beginning to listen to yourself. You alone are in charge of your own life and you alone are able to create it, so it is up to you to start listening to your intuition, trusting that you know what is right for you and enjoying your own company.

To show faith in yourself, first learn to enjoy your own company. Start doing things because you want to do them. Support yourself and back your own decisions rather than looking for admiration or respect from other people. Think about when you last did something for yourself. Didn't you feel that you were in charge – that you knew what you were doing and could trust yourself?

Know that what you want to do is great – and that's enough. You don't have to look to other people for support and reassurance – you don't have to sell yourself to anyone else. Solve your own problems – there's no need to ask anyone else for help. Make the approval of others less important than your own approval of yourself. Accept your own power and use it.

Me, Myself, I

You may already know what you enjoy doing alone (e.g. listening to music, shopping, roller-blading, reading, watching football etc), but you may feel that even those things are more fun in company. Get curious about what you really enjoy doing on your own, so you know what will uplift you if you are feeling low – without seeking the comfort of others.

Enjoy standing on your own two feet. Begin to value being alone with yourself.

Things I really like doing on my own :

Keep adding to this list

Becoming Confident

None of us is confident in all fields. You may feel confident in your intellectual and athletic prowess, for example, and yet under-confident in your appearance and relationships – or the other way round.

In the areas in which you don't feel confident you tend to avoid taking risks because you don't expect to be successful. You rely on the approval of others in order to feel good about yourself and yet at the same time you discount or ignore compliments that are paid to you.

Setting goals about any issues around your family will already have begun to make you feel better. It's now time to think about how you can become genuinely confident.

When you feel confident :

- you trust your own abilities
- you don't even contemplate the idea of failure
- you are positive, but realistic, about yourself and your situation
- you have a general sense that you are in control of that aspect of your life
- you believe that, within reason, you will be able to do what you want
- even when something goes wrong, you remain positive and accepting of yourself

And that may well be one of the key issues of self-confidence – when you feel self-confident you don't have to have approval in order to be accepted. You accept yourself.

Lack of self-confidence is not necessarily related to lack of ability, so it is something you can change.

How To Become More Confident

Before you start thinking about how to become more confident, I'd like you to consider what advantages there are in being *under*-confident. In other words, why you might choose to *remain* under-confident. You may see advantages other than those below. Discover your own.

3 possible advantages of remaining under-confident

1 Feeling safer

As an under-confident person you won't be expected to try anything new and if you don't try anything new you won't have to 'fail'. For confident people, that failure is an opportunity to learn, but for the under-confident it's yet another dent in an already fragile confidence.

2 No responsibility

Another benefit is that you get looked after. 'I'm so hopeless at DIY' means you'll get lots of people reassuring you, saying 'Don't worry, I'm hopeless too – it is difficult to assemble flatpack furniture' (for example) and you may even get a friend who says 'I'll look after you' and assembles your table.

3 Desire to remain modest

That incredibly big-headed person you once met who showed off all evening wasn't confident – s/he was showing off. Those who brag about their abilities are often the least confident. People with true confidence are usually genuinely modest and don't think there is anything special about their abilities. Think about the areas in which you feel confident – I'm sure you don't show off in those areas at all. You don't need to.

First think about all the advantages there are for you in being under-confident and see how important they really are to you. Being confident doesn't necessarily mean assembling your own table. It does mean looking forward to having a go – taking another step on your path to changing your life.

boosting my confidence

Confidence-boosting hints

- **Be yourself.** Forget trying to make others approve of you. Friends will love you even if they don't approve of everything you do, just as you love them and forgive their faults

- **Avoid exaggerating your negatives.** If you're not totally brilliant at something, it doesn't mean that you're a total failure

- **Don't allow something small to put you off your dreams.** If you fail your driving test or get refused when you ask someone out, just have another go

- **Give yourself credit for everything you do.** Begin to feel more confident with each thing you try. Every experience is an opportunity to learn – and, if you don't succeed, learn again from your mistakes. Taking risks will feed your self-confidence

- **Use positive affirmations in areas that you feel under-confident.** Using carefully chosen affirmations will help you change your feelings about yourself

- **Talk positively about yourself.** Labelling yourself 'loser', 'hopeless', 'stupid' etc., even in jest, can be self-fulfilling prophesies

- **Trust your intuition to guide you, not the opinions of others.** Once you trust yourself your confidence will grow

- **Lift yourself up.** Tap into things that have made you feel good before, such as listening to music or watching a video of Olympic rowers. Find out what raises your energy and empowers you – and enjoy it

Using Compliments

Think about what compliments you would enjoy receiving and what compliments would embarrass you. Maybe you can even remember some compliments you have been given that have embarrassed you, because you can't believe they're genuine.

In the future use the 'embarrassing' compliments as positive affirmations to enhance your self-confidence. For example, if you have had a compliment about your beautiful hair and you don't like your hair, affirm twice a day to yourself in front of the mirror 'My hair is beautiful – it really suits me' until you begin to believe it – others do.

Compliments I would enjoy and have received and would believe in

1 ....

2 ....

3 ....

Compliments I would – and have been – embarrassed to receive

1 ....

2 ....

3 ....

Embarrassing compliment I'm going to use as positive affirmation

....

....

....

....

You Are Your Own Hero

There are many life coaching exercises that will help you boost your confidence. One of them is to become aware that you already have the qualities that you have always admired in your heroes.

Listen to the You Are Your Own Hero talk on our website (www.affordablelifecoaching.org) now. You will hear how you are already on the path to being whatever you want to be.

You already embody the qualities that you admire and revere in others. The very reason that you may identify humour, for example, as a quality that Winston Churchill has, is that humour is a quality that is already an integral part of your personality. It may not be as fully developed as you'd like – but it's there. Someone else might describe Churchill as having been brave or intelligent. Those are qualities that would describe them. You don't have to look to others to find examples of people you admire – without knowing it, you are already your own hero.

Find heroes and use them to inspire you

- You don't have to admire your heroes for all the things they do. Work out exactly what it is about each of them that you most respect.
- Find your own heroes – from family, friends and colleagues. Study them and other confident people. Notice what they do that makes an impact. Could you incorporate that quality into your personality?
- Ask someone you know who you feel is wiser than you are, if they'd be willing to be your mentor. They'd probably be flattered and pleased.
- It's often easier to study literary characters that impress you as they are well described. When you read a novel or biography work out what it is, if anything, about the character that you respect. Those are qualities that you will find are already within you.

Perspectives

You can gain insight by imagining how different people or literary characters would handle a situation. It might be fun to be the confident Pollyanna (from the book of the same name), for example, at a party or Elizabeth Bennet (from *Pride and Prejudice*) at a job interview. Think who you would like to be in each of the following situations – or at least ask them for their advice.

Going for a job interview

1 ....

2 ....

3 ....

Starting a relationship

1 ....

2 ....

3 ....

At work

1 ....

2 ....

3 ....

Ending a relationship

1 ....

2 ....

3 ....

Next time you're in a stressful situation, ask yourself :

- How would this character see the situation I'm in?
- What thoughts would be running through their mind right now?
- How do I feel as them?
- How do I look and act as them?
- What might they say?
- What advice might they give me?

It's not acting. This perspectives game will take you into a new way of thinking and being – you'll find you know things that wouldn't otherwise occur to you.

Who Are Your Heroes?

1. Make a list of 5 people that you respect and admire

To make this list think about your past and the people you admired then and the present and people you admire now. This list could include members of your family, friends, colleagues, historical heroes, world leaders and fictional characters.

1 ....

2 ....

3 ....

4 ....

5 ....

2. Write down the qualities of each of your 'heroes'

Next to each of the names you have written down above, write the character qualities that you associate with each person – what you rate them for. It doesn't matter if several people have the same qualities.

3. Underline the qualities that appear more than once in your list.

Those are the qualities that are very important to you at the present time. See if you can't recognise them within yourself already.

4. Appreciate your qualities

From the list of qualities, now choose three which you had previously not recognised in yourself. From now on, resolve to find, focus on – and be proud of – these qualities in yourself.

1 ....

2 ....

3 ....

Confident Thinking

Positive (or confident) and negative thinking are both powerful thought patterns that will have a very strong influence on your life. Negative thoughts (like 'I can't') will stop you from achieving whatever is within your power to achieve. From now on, put your energy behind being positive and thinking confidently (and realistically), with lots of 'Yes' and 'I can' and 'I will'. Do something instead of holding back. If you feel confident and expect a positive outcome your life will change accordingly. It will take time, but when you change your thought patterns from negative to positive you will feel empowered to take positive actions, and you'll notice how good things start happening. You'll be trusting and loving yourself.

Of course, there are times in your life when things won't go well. You may break your leg, lose your job; friends or family may be ill or in trouble. There are events in life that you can't control, but none of them mean that you are a failure. To suffer is not to be a failure, it is part of being human. Even if there are dark threads running through the tapestry of your life, it's important to meet life with optimism and with a strength of purpose to find a new way through, rather than with pessimism. Expect that everything is working out for the best and then, when things go wrong, think positively, 'How do I deal with this? Let's find a way through that makes some sense of it all'. You know you can do it.

'There are always flowers for those who want to see them.'

Henri Matisse

I Love Myself

Fill this heart in with pictures of yourself as a small child or even teenager. In case you had any doubts, it will help you realise how wonderful you are.

I love …………………………………….. (write your name here)

Loving Yourself

Write down as many things as you can think of that you could do for yourself every day (or at least three times a week) that would show that you cared about yourself.

eg taking vitamins, giving up caffeine, going to bed earlier, drinking more water etc.

Write down as many things as you can think of that you could do once a fortnight to show how much you love yourself.

eg go to the cinema, buy yourself a bunch of flowers, have friends round for a bite to eat etc.

Loving Me is all about ...   being my own best friend
taking care of myself
focusing on me
being myself
finding my inner confidence
living my own life
moving on from my childhood
loving my family
listening to myself
accepting myself
becoming confident
acknowledging my qualities
appreciating my qualities
believing in myself
being optimistic
knowing I deserve it

taking care of me

6

taking care
of **me**

Your Balance Chart

When you love yourself it is natural to take care of yourself. But all of us have times when life gets on top of us, when it's good to be reminded of how to look after ourselves. Before beginning the next chapter about taking care of yourself, fill in and date this Balance Chart.

Look at your last few Balance Charts. What changes are you making?

Don't worry if your scores sometimes decrease before they go up again; this is all part of your growth process. Sometimes scores don't go right away in the direction you want them to. Use this as a reminder of how you want to live your life.

what changes am I making?

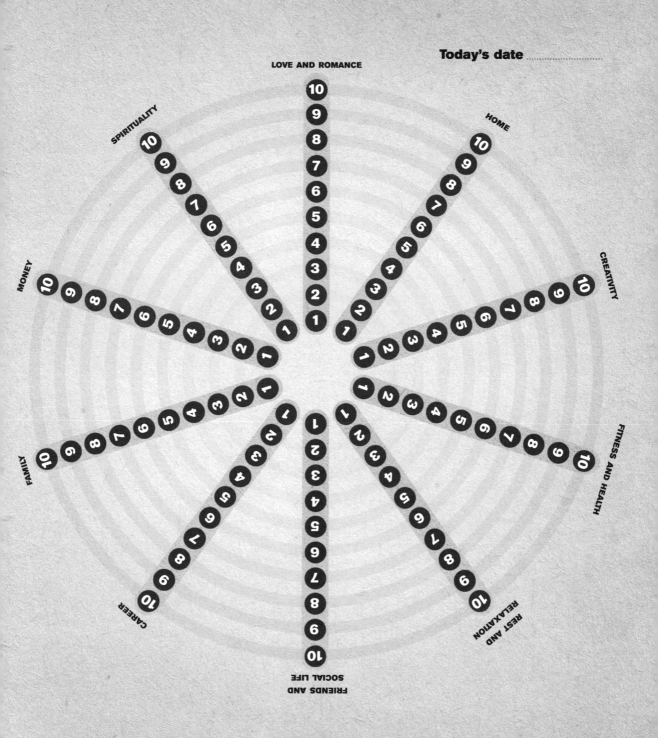

'Be a Friend
to thyself,
and others
will be so too.'

Thomas Fuller

De-Stressing

Taking care of yourself begins with understanding what makes you stressed. All of us experience stress or anxiety at some time or another, but some of us are more affected by it than others. Stress can be debilitating because if you are stressed you're not functioning properly and if you're not functioning properly then you become more stressed and so on. It's a vicious circle.

What can make you stressed

- change, both expected and unexpected – anything, from the death of a spouse to moving home
- putting pressure on yourself – having unrealistic expectations of what you can do
- money matters – from redundancy to winning the lottery
- relationships – from the in-laws, to work colleagues and neighbours
- not being heard or appreciated
- unmanageable feelings – especially in emotional crises
- being unable to say 'No' – you can end up giving so much of yourself to others that you have no time for you
- having too much to do – and not delegating
- not being able to switch off and relax – not even in bed at night
- making decisions – large or small
- minor hassles – from catching a train to public speaking to losing your keys to getting a parking ticket

Positive symptoms

Your body produces chemicals, such as adrenaline and noradrenaline, which help prepare it for an emergency. If these are produced at a moderate level, the stress will actually enable you to perform better by making you more alert and able to cope with your job interview or first public speaking performance.

Negative symptoms

If you start to produce these chemicals when they're not needed, such as in a busy office or an over-crowded train, you may begin to experience stress-related symptoms, such as headaches, nausea and indigestion.

Emotional symptoms

You can also experience emotional symptoms, like anxiety, fear, anger, frustration or depression. These feelings can feed on each other and themselves produce physical symptoms.

Behavioural symptoms

Your behaviour may change too. You may become withdrawn or indecisive. You may find you're not sleeping properly. You may be irritable or tearful. There may be a change in your eating and sexual habits and you may become physically or verbally aggressive – even if you were previously quite placid.

If you are prone to stress there are ways you can help yourself. Become aware of the first warning signs of stress – sudden feelings of anxiety or anger, extreme tiredness, feeling very tearful, getting run down and catching every cough and 'flu.

If you are feeling stressed ...

1. Calm yourself by slow, deep breathing

Start by taking a deep breath, hold this for a count of three and then slowly breathe out. Continue with this slow breathing until you feel more relaxed. Then you can carry on with what you were doing.

2. Take time out – even if it's only for five minutes

Time out for you may be getting a drink of water or walking around the block; it may be reading or exercising briefly or phoning a friend or shutting your eyes for a quick nap or meditation or taking a photograph. Experiment with what works for you.

What Can You Change?

This exercise is about reviewing your lifestyle
- Are you taking on too much?
- Could you delegate more?
- Could you do things in a more leisurely way?
- Could you prioritise more so you're not trying to do everything at once?
- Are your expectations of yourself realistic?
- Are you trying to change others?
- How much of your stress is caused by you?

Go through your Balance Chart, and for every one of the ten segments write at least two concerns that make you stressed. If you can't find anything to write in certain segments, write more in others.

Love & Romance

Home

Creativity

Health & Fitness

Rest & Relaxation

Friends & Social Life

Career

Family

Money

Spirituality

Divide the concerns you've just written down into three groups :

1. Those that will improve anyway over time – temporary worries.
2. Those that you can't do anything about – are they your problem?
3. Those that you can find a practical solution to.

Now delete everything you have written down that belong in the first and second groups and let go of those worries. Focus instead on those concerns that belong in group 3. You can do something about them. Work out what you're going to do – and when.

For each concern in group 3, ask yourself :

1. **What are the advantages to me in having this particular concern?** eg if going to parties makes me feel stressed, I can blame my lack of social life on the fact that I never go anywhere where I might meet new people

   ....

   ....

2. **What would stop this particular concern?** ....

   ....

3. **What actions (think of at least three) could I commit to that would help me with solving this particular concern?**

   ....

4. **Which of these actions appeals to me the most?** ....

   ....

5. **When and what am I going to do?** ....

   ....

   ....

6. **How will I feel when I've done it?** ....

   ....

Eat To Live

Food can make us feel fresh and healthy and give us energy; or it can make us feel bloated and lethargic. Watch babies and toddlers eating. They cry when they're hungry and spit out food they don't like. They eat as much as their bodies need and then they run away from the table – healthy and ready to go.

You may be out of touch with your body and eat when you're not hungry:

- Sitting behind a computer doesn't make you hungry – so you never experience complete satisfaction eating, because you're never hungry
- You're responding to hunger produced by your mind – a desire to recreate memories of pleasurable tastes
- You cover your food with spices and additives so it tempts your tastebuds – or you stimulate them with alcohol
- You may have been forced to finish your plate of food as a child
- Food is an easy way to satisfy your desires for pleasure – you use food to hide the emptiness in your life

Relearn that food is fuel. Only eat when you feel really hungry. Begin to eat consciously:

- Always sit down to eat and relax when eating – even when alone
- Breathe deeply 3 times before eating – become aware of your meal
- Slow down – deliberately chew each mouthful many times
- Eat mindfully and appreciatively – use your eyes as well as your mouth
- Let your body guide you to healthy choices
- If you begin to hurry up and finish your meal you have already lost some of your conscious awareness around the food

Get back in touch with what your body wants. Make changes slowly – that way they are easier to stick to. Before long you will notice eating becoming a deeper and more fulfilling experience. You will find true contentment rather than instant gratification. You will be honouring your body.

15 Healthy Eating Tips

1. Buy simple, whole, natural foods, rather than processed
2. Eat a balanced diet – include complex carbohydrates (such as wholemeal bread and jacket potatoes) to help your mood swings
3. Keep sugar and salt intake to a minimum
4. Eat at least 5 portions of fresh fruit and vegetables a day – these can help prevent colds and flu (ailments you often get when you're run down)
5. Monitor which foods work for you and which don't
6. Select food you know will energise you
7. Avoid foods that will make you feel sluggish
8. Always sit down to eat – even if it's only a snack
9. Don't do anything else when you eat – even talking with your mouth full can affect your digestion
10. Cook for yourself and others with love and an awareness of what you are cooking
11. Eat only when you are hungry – as a guideline, your stomach is the size of both your hands cupped together
12. Stop eating when you're still a little bit hungry
13. Drink plenty of water to rehydrate your body – but either before or after your meal, rather than during
14. Replace cups of coffee and tea with glasses of water or herbal tea (the effects of caffeine on the body can be similar to the effects of stress and anxiety)
15. Alcohol, junk food and smoking may appear to reduce tension, but will exacerbate the problem

Listen to your body – you used to.

‘Hunger is the
best pickle’

Benjamin Franklin

Conscious Eating

Your diet affects the way you feel about yourself, your fitness, your ability to sleep well at night and be full of energy during the day. Diet even affects your relationships – if you feel sluggish and not at one with your body, you won't bring much to any relationship.

Think about your eating habits (include drinking and smoking) and use the LIFE Model to see what you would like to change about them – and how to do it. The questions used are examples of the sort of questions you might want to ask. If they don't fit, choose your own.

LIVING : Analysis of current situation
Would I like to change anything about my current eating/drinking/smoking habits?

....

....

What have I tried so far?

....

....

What would I do if I knew I couldn't fail?

....

....

How badly do I want to change this habit?

....

....

IDEAL : Objectives
What would my ideal goal be? What do I want to achieve?

....

Is my goal realistic? Is it within my capabilities?

....

What's a realistic time scale for change?

....

FUEL : Improvement opportunities
What help and resources from others will I want to achieve my goal?

....

What could I do differently in order to achieve my ideal?

....

What could stop me achieving my ideal?

....

What would happen if I did nothing?

....

What could I do as a first step towards my goal?

....

ENERGY : Set a date
When and where will I take this first step?

....

How will I feel when I've done it?

....

My Food Diary

For a week, increase your awareness

1. Each time you eat or drink something, write down what you are eating and drinking as you do it – don't wait until the end of the day
2. Write down why you are eating – are you hungry, bored, sad, frustrated, happy, wanting a break, being sociable?
3. Write down a description of how you're feeling at the end of each meal – sleepy, bloated, energetic, ready to go?
4. Then note how you feel an hour later – still energetic or have you collapsed with a headache or a desire to sleep?

At the end of the week, check your diary

1. To see how balanced your diet is
2. To see whether you are eating too much or too little
3. To see if you feel more energetic eating many small meals in the day or three larger ones and what your optimum times to eat are
4. To see which foods energise you.

We often forget about healthy food we like and grab something instant to eat. In the space below write a list of all the healthy foods you enjoy eating. Keep adding to the list and use it for inspiration the next time you're stuck for ideas.

....

....

....

....

....

....

' Thou should'st
eat to live; not
live to eat.'

Cicero

Date   **My Food Diary: Day 1**

....

What I'm eating/drinking   **Time**

What am I eating for?

The food/drink is making me feel

1 hour later: How do I feel?

....

What I'm eating/drinking   **Time**

What am I eating for?

The food/drink is making me feel

1 hour later: How do I feel?

....

What I'm eating/drinking   **Time**

What am I eating for?

The food/drink is making me feel

1 hour later: How do I feel?

....

What I'm eating/drinking   **Time**

What am I eating for?

The food/drink is making me feel

1 hour later: How do I feel?

What I'm eating/drinking   **Time**

What am I eating for?

The food/drink is making me feel

1 hour later: How do I feel?

What I'm eating/drinking   **Time**

What am I eating for?

The food/drink is making me feel

1 hour later: How do I feel?

What I'm eating/drinking   **Time**

What am I eating for?

The food/drink is making me feel

1 hour later: How do I feel?

why am I eating?

My Food Diary: Day 2

Date

What I'm eating/drinking   **Time**

What am I eating for?

The food/drink is making me feel

1 hour later: How do I feel?

What I'm eating/drinking   **Time**

What am I eating for?

The food/drink is making me feel

1 hour later: How do I feel?

What I'm eating/drinking   **Time**

What am I eating for?

The food/drink is making me feel

1 hour later: How do I feel?

What I'm eating/drinking   **Time**

What am I eating for?

The food/drink is making me feel

1 hour later: How do I feel?

What I'm eating/drinking   **Time**

What am I eating for?

The food/drink is making me feel

1 hour later: How do I feel?

What I'm eating/drinking   **Time**

What am I eating for?

The food/drink is making me feel

1 hour later: How do I feel?

What I'm eating/drinking   **Time**

What am I eating for?

The food/drink is making me feel

1 hour later: How do I feel?

what am I eating?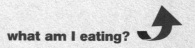

My Food Diary: Day 3

What I'm eating/drinking   **Time**

What am I eating for?

The food/drink is making me feel

1 hour later: How do I feel?

What I'm eating/drinking   **Time**

What am I eating for?

The food/drink is making me feel

1 hour later: How do I feel?

What I'm eating/drinking   **Time**

What am I eating for?

The food/drink is making me feel

1 hour later: How do I feel?

What I'm eating/drinking   **Time**

What am I eating for?

The food/drink is making me feel

1 hour later: How do I feel?

What I'm eating/drinking   **Time**

What am I eating for?

The food/drink is making me feel

1 hour later: How do I feel?

What I'm eating/drinking   **Time**

What am I eating for?

The food/drink is making me feel

1 hour later: How do I feel?

What I'm eating/drinking   **Time**

What am I eating for?

The food/drink is making me feel

1 hour later: How do I feel?

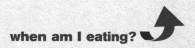

when am I eating?

My Food Diary: Day 4

Date

....

What I'm eating/drinking   **Time**

What am I eating for?

The food/drink is making me feel

1 hour later: How do I feel?

....

What I'm eating/drinking   **Time**

What am I eating for?

The food/drink is making me feel

1 hour later: How do I feel?

....

What I'm eating/drinking   **Time**

What am I eating for?

The food/drink is making me feel

1 hour later: How do I feel?

....

What I'm eating/drinking   **Time**

What am I eating for?

The food/drink is making me feel

1 hour later: How do I feel?

What I'm eating/drinking   **Time**

What am I eating for?

The food/drink is making me feel

1 hour later: How do I feel?

What I'm eating/drinking   **Time**

What am I eating for?

The food/drink is making me feel

1 hour later: How do I feel?

What I'm eating/drinking   **Time**

What am I eating for?

The food/drink is making me feel

1 hour later: How do I feel?

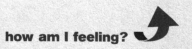

how am I feeling?

Date   **My Food Diary: Day 5**

....

What I'm eating/drinking   **Time**

What am I eating for?

The food/drink is making me feel

1 hour later: How do I feel?

....

What I'm eating/drinking   **Time**

What am I eating for?

The food/drink is making me feel

1 hour later: How do I feel?

....

What I'm eating/drinking   **Time**

What am I eating for?

The food/drink is making me feel

1 hour later: How do I feel?

....

What I'm eating/drinking   **Time**

What am I eating for?

The food/drink is making me feel

1 hour later: How do I feel?

What I'm eating/drinking   **Time**

What am I eating for?

The food/drink is making me feel

1 hour later: How do I feel?

What I'm eating/drinking   **Time**

What am I eating for?

The food/drink is making me feel

1 hour later: How do I feel?

What I'm eating/drinking   **Time**

What am I eating for?

The food/drink is making me feel

1 hour later: How do I feel?

how are my energy levels?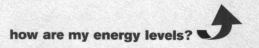

Date

My Food Diary: Day 6

What I'm eating/drinking .... **Time**

What am I eating for?

The food/drink is making me feel

1 hour later: How do I feel?

What I'm eating/drinking .... **Time**

What am I eating for?

The food/drink is making me feel

1 hour later: How do I feel?

What I'm eating/drinking .... **Time**

What am I eating for?

The food/drink is making me feel

1 hour later: How do I feel?

What I'm eating/drinking .... **Time**

What am I eating for?

The food/drink is making me feel

1 hour later: How do I feel?

What I'm eating/drinking   **Time**

What am I eating for?

The food/drink is making me feel

1 hour later: How do I feel?

What I'm eating/drinking   **Time**

What am I eating for?

The food/drink is making me feel

1 hour later: How do I feel?

What I'm eating/drinking   **Time**

What am I eating for?

The food/drink is making me feel

1 hour later: How do I feel?

am I changing my eating habits?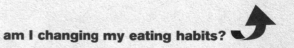

Date

My Food Diary: Day 7

What I'm eating/drinking   **Time**

What am I eating for?

The food/drink is making me feel

1 hour later: How do I feel?

What I'm eating/drinking   **Time**

What am I eating for?

The food/drink is making me feel

1 hour later: How do I feel?

What I'm eating/drinking   **Time**

What am I eating for?

The food/drink is making me feel

1 hour later: How do I feel?

What I'm eating/drinking   **Time**

What am I eating for?

The food/drink is making me feel

1 hour later: How do I feel?

What I'm eating/drinking   **Time**

What am I eating for?

The food/drink is making me feel

1 hour later: How do I feel?

What I'm eating/drinking   **Time**

What am I eating for?

The food/drink is making me feel

1 hour later: How do I feel?

What I'm eating/drinking   **Time**

What am I eating for?

The food/drink is making me feel

1 hour later: How do I feel?

time to start working out

Feeling Fit

Physical exercise can relieve stress too – even walking to the shops. If you feel you're fit enough already, then you probably are. If you don't, start becoming conscious of your body. Not only conscious of what you are eating, but also conscious of how you are moving and whether your body is in top form. Make it this week to have any health check-ups that you've been putting off, such as the dentist.

Using the LIFE Model will help you work out how to achieve your fitness goal. The questions are to inspire you. You can keep the format of the LIFE Model and ask your own questions as well if you want to.

LIVING : Analysis of where I am now
How healthy and fit am I?

....

....

What would I like to change about my health and fitness?

....

....

What have I done so far about this situation? What have I tried?

....

....

What would I do if I knew I couldn't fail?

....

....

IDEAL : My goals

Remember when I last felt in peak condition – exercising hard, sleeping soundly, jumping out of bed in the morning, feeling strong – as if I could climb Everest. Think about how it felt.

What effect would it have on my life if I achieved my fitness goal?

....

....

Is this goal realistic? Is it within my capabilities?

....

....

FUEL : My improvement opportunities
How am I going to set about making the changes?

....

....

Who (or what) could help me with these changes?

....

....

What am I going to do as a first step?

....

ENERGY : Going for it
When and where am I going to take this first step?

....

How will I feel when I've done it?

....

R&R

You know how grumpy, volatile and sometimes even tearful you feel when you haven't had enough sleep. Sleep and rest are essential for a calm, de-stressed life and yet sleeping problems are common when you're suffering from stress.

If you can't sleep easily, try to :

- Stick to a bed-time routine to calm you down. Meditate or have a hot bath (with or without lavender oil and candles) before bed
- Clear your head by writing down a list of everything that you want to do the next day (or any worries you have), then putting a final line underneath the list before you go to sleep
- Avoid caffeine altogether, but especially in the evening
- Read a classic novel before sleep – television, magazines, newspapers and gripping novels can act as stimulants
- Sleep without alcohol. The quality of your sleep will be better
- Get cosy. Are your mattress and bedcovers comfortable? Is your room the correct temperature for you?
- Change anything in your bedroom that annoys you – including moving out your partner if they snore, or getting earplugs
- Eyeshades can help with noise and light
- If you can't sleep at night, have a power nap during the day. Lie down holding a bunch of keys in your hand over the edge of the bed or sofa. When you drop off to sleep, your grip will loosen and the noise of the keys clattering to the floor will wake you up. That split second of sleep will be enough to revive you for the rest of the day. Enjoy relaxing – build it into your timetable, don't feel guilty about it. Read, practise yoga, meditate, take up a hobby or go to an evening class. Spend time on you. Make time for going on holiday and having clear weekends where you can unwind as much as possible. It will re-charge you.

One of the best antidotes for stress is enjoying yourself. Bring some fun into your life. Even simple treats like a brief walk, watching a funny sitcom or cooking a healthy meal can help you deal with stress. Noticing what helps you relax and what you enjoy will be useful for the rest of your life.

Relaxing

Without thinking, write down 5 things that help you relax.
It may be drinking a glass of wine or going for a ride or chatting to friends or lying in the sun or sleeping.

1. ....

2. ....

3. ....

4. ....

5. ....

In order to build at least one of these relaxing treats into your life, what will you have to give up?

Go to bed half-an-hour earlier than usual every day this week and notice what effect it has.

It's often said about babies: 'the more they sleep, the more they sleep'. You may not be able to sleep half an hour earlier than usual, but if you are relaxing in bed for the thirty minutes before sleep you can often get to sleep more easily. Why not read or listen to some soothing music – classical, jazz or gentle ballads. Start a good book – or finish an on-going one. Take bedtime at a leisurely pace.

Home Sweet Home

There are many reasons for feeling dissatisfied with your home. It could be that you're in temporary accommodation and sharing too small a space with people you don't like. It could be that within your own home you don't have a space of your own, or that you don't like the neighbourhood you're living in. It could be that your home is too expensive and the costs worry you or that you live alone and would prefer not to.

Even if you go out to work and spend large chunks of time socializing afterwards, your sleeping hours are spent in your home – and having a good night's sleep can be deeply affected by the atmosphere surrounding you. You want to feel comfortable in your home; to be able to laugh without shyness and cry without embarrassment and to feel the walls protecting you.

If you have decluttered your home, explored your neighbourhood and filled each room with love and fresh flowers and still don't feel happy – try to move. Home is where life begins.

taking care of me is all about …

understanding myself
avoiding stress
reviewing my lifestyle
being aware of my diet
learning to eat consciously
listening to my body
keeping track of my diet
getting fit and healthy
getting enough sleep
getting enough relaxation
having fun
enjoying my home

loving you

7

loving **you**

Your Balance Chart

You have learnt about loving and taking care of yourself. Now you are going to reach out to others. Before you start the next chapter on relationships, fill in the last Balance Chart in this book.

Is your Balance Chart developing the way you would like it to? Do you know what changes you have made to make it progress?

what changes will I make next?

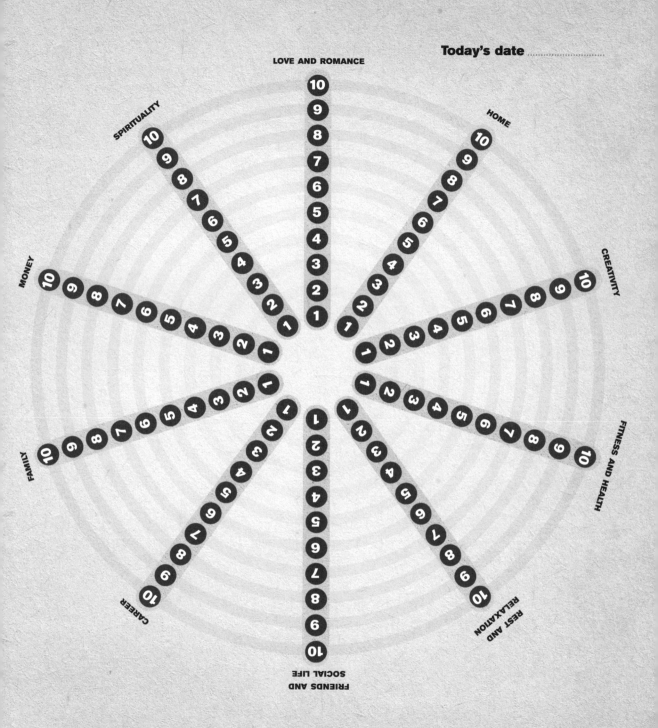

Today's date ....

The Ripple Effect

The ripple effect is about a stone being thrown into a pond. The ripples that are created by that one splash stretch out wider and wider across the pond affecting the whole of its surface. Your life is like that too – although you usually aren't aware of it. By your everyday actions, you will make a difference to many people's lives.

You may feel that if you don't reach celebrity status or become an aid worker or fireman there's little you can do to change the world or have an effect on it, but that's not true. You can ensure that in your own world you are having a positive impact on others.

That's the ripple effect in action. There is enormous power in using your life for others. If you can, build into your goals something for someone else too.

Making A Positive Impact

If you are a teacher you can see daily how you are passing on to others what you have learnt. If you are a parent you can see how you are creating future generations. But you don't have to be either to be part of the ripple effect.

Below write a list of the way you help others. First relate your actions to family members and friends and then to your colleagues and neighbours. You could also think how you already impact on strangers – or how you could. And, if you don't know your neighbours or colleagues, introduce yourself this week. Even a smile travels. Everything you do affects someone.

Family members   **How I help/inspire/impact on them**

Friends   **How I help/inspire/impact on them**

Colleagues   **How I help/inspire/impact on them**

Neighbours   **How I help/inspire/impact on them**

Listening Barriers

Another way to make a difference in people's lives is to listen to them – properly. Because if no one is listening, there is no communication. Tick any of the listening barriers you recognise in yourself. You may not use each of them all the time, but many of them may be familiar. Review this list again after a month of practising conscious listening and notice how you've changed.

10 Reasons I stop listening   **Tick here**

1. **I 'know' what they're going to say**
    and don't think it'll be interesting   ◯

2. **I'm preoccupied with something else**
    I think about my worry and don't listen to theirs   ◯

3. **Too much information is being given to me**
    I wanted them to agree with me, not bore me with detail   ◯

4. **I'm too busy thinking what I want to say next**
    I'm not listening, I'm constructing my next speech   ◯

5. **I'm self-referencing**
    I want to tell them my (more interesting) story   ◯

6. **I'm thinking about what advice to give them**
    I want to solve their problem, not listen to what it actually was ◯

7. **I love fighting or joking**
    I'm waiting for a flaw to attack or for a pause so I can tell a joke ◯

8. **I want people to like me so I agree with everything**
    I'm shaking my head and smiling, not listening and not involved   ◯

9. **I'm day-dreaming**
    Day-dreams block the other person out   ◯

10. **I don't understand**
    I don't want to appear stupid so I don't ask for clarification   ◯

To Listen

The Chinese pictogram of the verb *to listen* is made up of five parts.
It translates as *I give you my ears, my eyes, my undivided attention and
my heart.* Conscious listening is all that – and more.

You

Ear

Eyes

Undivided
attention

Heart

Conscious Listening

Half your conversational life is spent listening. You listen to everyone –
family, friends, colleagues, strangers. But how often are you really taking
in what they're saying? How often are you putting yourself in their place
and hearing the meaning beyond the words.

Conscious listening is being interested in what the other person is
thinking, feeling and wanting to tell you. It's effective and active
listening and involves checking that you really did understand what the
other person was saying.

Conscious listening includes :
- fully concentrating on another
- carefully listening to their feelings
- letting them finish before you begin to talk
- giving a very brief summary of what they said
- asking questions if you're not sure you've understood
- allowing them to feel understood and acknowledged

When you listen consciously, you maintain eye contact and actively
focus your attention on what's being said. You keep your emotions
under control so that you can understand and accept what the other
person is saying for what it is, independent of your feelings about it.

3 Advantages of conscious listening :
1. You can hear, feel and understand another's viewpoint – even if you
   don't agree with it
2. Both of you relax – knowing your messages & feelings are being heard
3. Once you are both relaxed, you have more attention for listening

Who Listens To Me?

Why conscious listening?

- It defuses the situation if the other person is angry, hurt or expressing difficult feelings
- It identifies areas of agreement so areas of disagreement are put in perspective and diminished rather than magnified
- It helps others spot the flaws in their reasoning when they hear their argument played back to them without criticism
- Once people feel acknowledged they can back down or consider alternatives without losing face

Write a list below of all the people who listen to you. Then think about how you can tell they've really listened to you.

Everyone who listens to me　　**How I can tell they've listened**

1. ....　　...

2. ....　　...

3. ....　　...

4. ....　　...

5. ....　　...

How can people tell you've listened?

....

Evaluating Friends

It takes time to make a true friendship. You can have many acquaintances, but the deep understanding between two friends is a rare and special commodity to be treasured. There isn't always much time for social life, so it is important to make time for those friendships you value – especially if your friend needs you to be there for them. It's also good to be open to new friendships – one can meet people one gels with at any stage of one's life.

Friends usually divide into two groups – those who energise, and those who drain you and, although it may sound brutal, those who wear you out and leave you feeling grumpy, frustrated and depressed may have to be weeded out. Even if you have known them a long time, it doesn't mean you want to keep on seeing them. It may be time for them to make way for those friends – old or new – who make you laugh and feel good about yourself.

Think about everyone that you've considered to be a friend in the last 2 years. Write down their names in one or other of the two columns below:

Friends who energise you   **Friends who drain you**

....

....

....

....

....

....

Pick up the phone and call one of the friends who energise you now. Arrange to see them soon. Then, pick up the phone and call another.

'If a man does not make new acquaintance as he advances through life, he will soon find himself left alone. A man, Sir, should keep his friendship in constant repair.'

Samuel Johnson

Falling In Love

As well as friends you love, there is true love. At the start of a romantic relationship, all you can see is the compatibility between the two of you. You are both attentive, biddable – a unit. You notice how perfectly you harmonise together and how he/she fits all your criteria.

What goes wrong?

- When you first met, did you project what you wanted to see onto him/her?
- Do you both gradually begin to reveal aspects of your character that at first you kept hidden?
- Do you begin to see things you chose to ignore when you first met?
- Do you both change over time?

Ironically it is only when the scales fall from your eyes and you become aware that your partner is another human being – and not a fairy tale character – that you can start to experience a meaningful and conscious relationship and begin to love, rather than be 'in love'.

A Conscious Relationship is when you ...

- realise you can't change your partner – only yourself
- can see the part you play in the relationship and can take responsibility for it
- don't blame your partner for something you don't like, but instead realise how you are feeling and that it's your responsibility
- can set the boundaries for what you want and don't want in the relationship (keep checking that the boundaries are still relevant)
- can understand, acknowledge and honestly admit your feelings
- can work together

Conscious Relationships

Make a list of all the important people in your life. They could be lovers, partners, friends, family members, colleagues, neighbours etc. Aim for at least four people.

Names

1. ....

....

2. ....

....

3. ....

....

4. ....

....

5. ....

....

6. ....

....

7. ....

....

8. ....

....

....

Now, next to each of these names, write down a couple of aspects of their character you would like to change – things that annoy you.

Look carefully at the list of annoyances you just wrote. Are they things you would like to change about yourself?

Enjoying You

Take 5 minutes and as quickly as possible finish this sentence:
The things I do NOT want to change in my relationship with

.... (insert name of partner)

are ... .

....

....

Now take 5 minutes and write spontaneously:
All the ways in which I get frustrated with

.... (insert name of partner

are ... .

....

....

In both cases, substitute your previous partner or a close friend or family member if you are not currently in a relationship.

Even if your relationship is rock solid, writing the first list feels challenging, possibly because you assume it will to be easy to answer. The things you don't want to change are often values like trust or frankness or emotions like warmth, security and humour that can be hard to find words for.

No matter how loving your relationship with your partner is, you may have found it quite easy to write lists and lists of the ways in which you find your partner frustrating.

Are these frustrating things serious or trivial? Are they your issues or your partner's? Go down the list and tick all the issues that are yours.

'They do not love
that do not show
their love.'

William Shakespeare

Am I In The Right Relationship?

Until you love yourself and know what you're worth, you can't expect anyone else to. In order to change the way your partner treats you, you have to change the way you treat yourself because your relationships are a reflection of you and your state of mind.

If you don't feel worthy of a good relationship, you'll put up with unacceptable behaviour, so if at any stage in a relationship you are thinking :

- is this right or wrong for me?
- is it me or him/her that's right?
- do I want to do what he/she says?
- why am I doing this?
- is it because he/she wants me to?

Trust your intuition and do what you feel to be right. If you want help tapping into your intuition, then the LIFE Model will help you to decide what you want from this relationship, where your boundaries are and how to stick to them. Make up your own questions as well.

L for LIVING (where I am now in this relationship)
What would I like to change about my present relationship?

....

....

What have I tried to change in the past?

....

....

I for IDEAL (what I would like from this relationship)
What would my ideal relationship be?

....

....

Is this realistic or what would I have to do to make it realistic?

....

....

F for FUEL (who and what can help me succeed)
What help will I want in order to achieve this ideal relationship?

....

What could I do differently?

....

....

Who (or what) could stop me achieving this ideal relationship?

....

....

E for ENERGY (going for it)
What is my next step?

....

When, where and how will I do it?

....

How will I feel when I've done it?

....

....

Growing Together

All relationships have their ups and downs and there may be times when you wonder what on earth you're doing together. But growing together with your partner can be a deeply rewarding experience – sharing a life. Supporting each other as you grow as individuals – and taking time to grow together.

Invest time in your relationship

- spend time together
- appreciate each other
- care for each other
- surprise each other
- share new experiences together
- encourage each other's individuality
- boost each other's confidence
- discuss the future
- introduce them to the things you love
- do things together
- make time for each other
- be honest
- be curious about them
- be alone together
- make life easier for them
- talk about everything
- relax together
- see life from their point of view as well as your own
- tell them what you enjoy (and what you don't)
- laugh (and cry) together
- be two individuals who enjoy being together
- express your love for each other

Show your love

Show those in your life how much you love them. Give them at least five hugs a day. Notice how it makes you feel.

Loving You is all about ...

the ripple effect
listening consciously
communicating
enjoying others
relating
trusting my intuition
setting boundaries
having fun
growing together
showing my affection

what next?

What Next?

How do you feel now you've reached the end of *The Big Book of Me*? Did you get out of it what you had hoped to – or even more? Have you changed in the way you wanted to – or in different ways that you had never expected to? What about your dream for the future – is it still the same or has it blossomed and grown to suit the bigger, more beautiful you?

One of the things life coaching is designed to do is to stimulate you into changing patterns both mental and physical that you've had for many years and replacing them with new, positive ones. Now that you have worked through *The Big Book of Me*, you will have become more aware of yourself and will have begun to notice how and what you are changing.

These changes may include :
- knowing what is unique about you
- increased self-confidence
- an appreciation of what you already have
- an understanding of what you want
- a desire to take control of your life
- becoming more aware of your role in the world

Changing your life can take time, but once you're committed to change you'll notice how all sorts of things conspire to help you. Enjoy each experience that comes your way. And stay curious – about everything.

Affordable Life Coaching

The Big Book of Me is based on the Affordable Life Coaching course which I designed and wrote, and on my observations of what triggered change in those who attended my group. I hope it will trigger the same positive changes in you.

I've always loved helping others discover their unique purpose in life. But, when I first started out, doing something that came so easily to me didn't seem a challenging enough career. I went for my other love – graphic design and worked first as a designer and later as an author of twelve how-to books. I still helped friends with their lives on an ad hoc basis, but I was not working professionally as a 'life changer' – and, ironically, I was not really happy with my own career.

It was only after the birth of my fourth child that I decided I wanted to work as a life coach – empowering others to live a life they wanted to live, but didn't feel they knew how to. I trained as a coach and realised I was finally really enjoying my own career. I had come home.

Life Coaching is extremely rewarding for both the coach and the coachee – but it's usually very expensive. I started Affordable Life Coaching in 2004 feeling that there must be a way of having all the positive results of coaching for less money. Running groups seemed to me a perfect solution. Rather than working one-to-one, I could coach groups of people, thus reducing cost. The group would also have masses of other advantages – the sharing of ideas, support within the group, meeting new people, networking and general reinforcement. Living in England I was aware that privacy was an issue. Few people want to share their dreams or concerns with others (at least not at first), so Affordable Life Coaching had to allow people to be private, wherever possible – with everyone working on their own within the group, but being able to share if they wanted to.

I ran my first group in my home, starting with an e-mail to my address book asking anyone who was interested in changing their life (or at least a part of it) to come along. The invitation included the Socrates quote 'The unexamined life is not worth living', which, I felt, summed my concept up. We were going to be examining and developing our lives.

The first sessions saw a lot of changes. The early groups began with the filling in of the Balance Chart, followed by a talk and supper. After a few months, with much feedback from coachees and visiting coaches, the final format of the sessions emerged.

An Affordable Life Coaching session now consists of :
- Coachees discussing their previous week's goal with each other
- Coachees writing down their previous week's achievements
- Coachees deciding on their goal for the following week
- Inspirational talk by coach (covering a different topic each week)
- Coaching work (much like the exercises in this book)
- Choosing one thing each coachee will take away from this session

Covering a different topic every week is one of the things that makes Affordable Life Coaching different from one-to-one life coaching. It becomes a self-development process, with exploration into parts of your life that you might never otherwise have thought about. It's a weekly time to get curious about you and your life and, as such, is an invaluable experience.

Although we started our groups in the United Kingdom, I believe that everybody should be able to be coached. In order to achieve this dream Affordable Life Coaching has just started to offer both one-to-one and tele-coaching for anybody, no matter where they are based. In one-to-one we provide clients with personal coaches. In tele-coaching we hold an Affordable Life Coaching session over the telephone for as many participants as want to join in from anywhere in the world.

I've had so many advisors and helpers along the way to whom I am totally indebted. Affordable Life Coaching has evolved and grown effortlessly. I've trusted that this business will work and be able to help people everywhere and, so far, everything has fallen into place. Life Coaching is a wonderful way of empowering and inspiring others. Seeing coachees getting in touch with themselves and becoming confident enough to do what they have discovered they want to do is exciting to watch. I have been so lucky and am so grateful. Thank you.

If you've enjoyed *The Big Book of Me*, come along and experience a group. As well as offering the fun of working with other people, the exercises are different from the ones here, so it will be a new experience. Coming to one of our groups is one of the most enjoyable and satisfying ways to spend time – thinking about you.

Nina Grunfeld

Acknowledgments

Mentors

Annie Lionnet, Henry Morris, Lucy Sisman, Nicholas Underhill, Jane Whistler, Gill and Robin Yourston – and my children

Coaches

Jilla Bond, Christine Chalkin, Mia Forbes-Pirie, Pauline Gillman, Philippa Heseltine, Maurits Kalff, Geraldine Kelly, Gordon Melvin, Daniel Smart, Bea Sullivan, Alex Szabo and anyone else who has since expressed an interest in Affordable Life Coaching

The First Affordable Life Coaching Group

Yael Azulay, Eleanor Bentall, Adrea Blakeney, Lis Bosman, Mia Cameron, Philip and Sally Cleary, Zoe du Boulay, Nicola Ellis, Catherine Fellowes, Kate Flint, Claire Gardner, Sophie Humbert, Elaine Jackson, Jenny James, Majka Kaiser, Peggy King, Marleen Krishnan, Mags Mackean, Felicity McInnes, Vivi Mellegard, Tamsin Mitchell, Vanessa Muir-Smith, Nina Rajan, Karen Sparks, Hilary Speller, Granville Stephenson, Jonathan Swain, Julia Valdambrini,

Title

Graham Dick, Sally Marlow, Hugo Stanley, Ursula and William Underhill

Designers

Cecilia Carey, Colourstat (Mick, Michael and Rob), Two Associates (David Eldridge, James Empringham, Rob Hackett)

Wordsmiths

Aurea Carpenter, Julia Booth-Clibborn, Craig Brown, Alice Carey, Frances Underhill, Frances Welch, Nick Welch

Help And Inspiration

Ann Barr, Britta Bielenberg, Adrian Brooks, Sarah Chalmers, Rosemary Cowan, Rosie de Lisle, Chrissie Dimitrov, Caroline Douglas, Matthew

Durdy, Leslie Elliott, Jeremy Gilbey, Mandy and Paul Grunfeld, Jacqueline Ivory, Maggie Kent, Margie Kinmonth, Marzena Koper, Janet Korris, Anna-Louise Parkinson, Pippa Parsons, Melissa Reaney, Dava Sagenkahn, Daisy Shann, Dasha Shenkman, all at Short Books, Emma Townsend, Thomas Underhill, William Ward, Roger Watson, Oenone Williams

Marketing
Claire Alexander, Lloyd Boman, Mel Carson, Alison Down, Francesca Goddard

PR
Lucinda Buxton, Angela Martin, Matthew Solon

Business Advice
Nick Alexander, Adrienne Carr, Reza Karim, Digby Trout, Tom Underhill

Computer
Andy Copper, Michael Underhill, James Wood

Fairy Godmother (and Publisher)
Rebecca Nicolson

For Thoughts, Doodles, Collages or Action Plans

For Thoughts, Doodles, Collages or Action Plans

For Thoughts, Doodles, Collages or Action Plans

For Thoughts, Doodles, Collages or Action Plans

For Thoughts, Doodles, Collages or Action Plans

For Thoughts, Doodles, Collages or Action Plans

For Thoughts, Doodles, Collages or Action Plans